D1398910

USA TODAY

HEALTH REPORTS:
DISEASES AND DISORDERS

LEUKEMIA

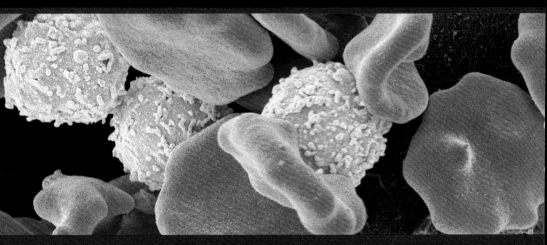

CONNIE GOLDSMITH

TWENTY-FIRST CENTURY BOOKS
MINNEAPOLIS

This book is dedicated to my father, Ernie, and his sister, my Aunt Iris, siblings who died of leukemia many years ago.

Cover image: This micrograph shows red blood cells (orange) and white blood cells (white) from a patient who has leukemia.

USA TODAY®, its logo, and associated graphics are federally registered trademarks. All rights are reserved. All USA TODAY text, graphics, and photographs are used pursuant to a license and may not be reproduced, distributed, or otherwise used without the express written consent of Gannett Co., Inc.

USA TODAY Snapshots®, graphics, and excerpts from USA TODAY articles on pages 8, 11, 16–17, 22–23, 36, 48–49, 56–57, 71, 76, 78, 95, 96, 99, 100–101, 102, 108 © copyright 2012 by USA TODAY.

Copyright © 2012 by Connie Goldsmith

All rights reserved. International copyright secured. No part of this book may be reproduced, stored in a retrieval system, or transmitted in any form or by any means—electronic, mechanical, photocopying, recording, or otherwise—without the prior written permission of Lerner Publishing Group, Inc., except for the inclusion of brief quotations in an acknowledged review.

Twenty-First Century Books
A division of Lerner Publishing Group, Inc.
241 First Avenue North
Minneapolis, MN 55401 U.S.A.

Website address: www.lernerbooks.com

Library of Congress Cataloging-in-Publication Data

Goldsmith, Connie, 1945–
    Leukemia / by Connie Goldsmith.
        p. cm. — (USA Today health reports: diseases and disorders)
    Includes bibliographical references and index.
    ISBN 978-0-7613-6087-2 (lib. bdg. : alk. paper)
    1. Leukemia—Juvenile literature.I. Title. II. Series.
  RC643.G63 2012
  616.99'419—dc22   2010046545

Manufactured in the United States of America
1 – MG – 7/15/11

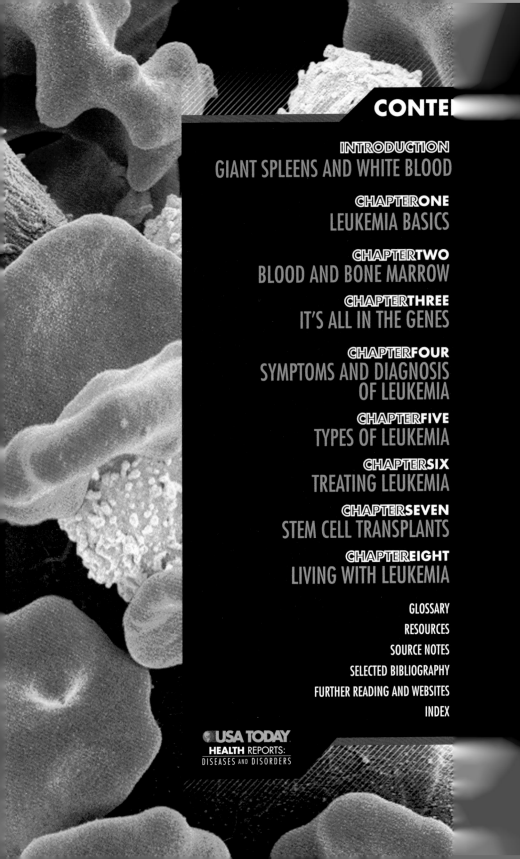

CONTENTS

USA TODAY
HEALTH REPORTS:
DISEASES AND DISORDERS

GIANT SPLEENS AND WHITE BLOOD

Leukemia is a cancer of the blood and the bone marrow, the soft spongy material that grows inside the large bones of the body. Healthy bone marrow produces just the right number and the right kind of white blood cells to help the body fight infection. Bone marrow also produces red blood cells that carry oxygen to every part of the body and platelets that help blood to clot. But when people develop leukemia, the cancerous bone marrow produces enormous numbers of abnormal, immature white blood cells. The sheer volume of these cancerous white blood cells means there is not room enough for normal red blood cells and platelets.

The decrease in red blood cells means that the body does not get enough oxygen. This leaves people feeling worn out and exhausted. The decrease in platelets means that the blood cannot clot properly. Leukemia patients often have many bruises, or they bleed a lot from a small cut. And because the white blood cells produced by cancerous bone marrow are abnormal, they cannot help the body fight off infections. People with leukemia are likely to get sick more often than healthy people because of the shortage of normal white blood cells.

CANCER IS AN OLD DISEASE

Human cancer has been around for thousands of years. Some ancient skeletons and the dried flesh of mummies show signs of cancer. Egyptian healers described cancer and how to treat it in two manuscripts written on papyrus in about 1600 B.C. These documents provide evidence of early Egyptian medicine.

Hippocrates, often called the father of medicine, lived in Greece between 460 B.C. and 370 B.C. He examined the bodies of people who had died of odd growths that he called tumors. He noticed that some tumors reached out with leglike protrusions, seeming to claw their way into surrounding organs and tissue. Hippocrates thought the tumors looked like crabs. He called them *karkinos*, Greek for "crabs." The word *cancer* comes from *karkinos*.

Most forms of cancer grow in solid lumps or tumors, making them easy to feel or to see on X-rays and other imaging studies. A woman feels a lump in her breast, and her doctor suspects breast cancer. A man coughs up blood, and his doctor discovers the shadow of lung cancer on an X-ray. A child has a seizure, and the doctor finds a brain tumor using a special type of brain scan.

LEUKEMIA — NO TUMORS

Leukemia does not cause tumors. There are no lumps to feel or masses to discover on an X-ray. So while leukemia has probably been around as long as other kinds of cancer, doctors didn't identify it until 1827. In that year, French physician Alfred Velpeau cut up and examined the body of a dead man. The man had suffered weakness and fever. The autopsy revealed that the man's blood was thin, pale, and filled with what Velpeau thought was pus. The dead man's spleen was twenty times larger than normal. The spleen is an abdominal organ that performs several jobs, including removing dead blood cells from circulation.

Other doctors autopsied people who had died with similar symptoms and discovered the same findings: greatly enlarged spleens and white "pus globules" floating in the blood. In 1845 Scottish physician John Bennett looked into his microscope and discovered that the puslike material was actually a huge number of white blood cells. That same year, Dr. Rudolph Virchow of Germany

USA TODAY

named the disease *weisses blut*, German for "white blood." Because medical terms generally come from Greek or Latin, weisses blut soon became known as leukemia, from the Greek words for white blood.

LEUKEMIA AND ITS VICTIMS

The American Cancer Society estimates that about 43,050 Americans developed leukemia in 2010. About 21,840 of those people died from their leukemia the same year. Although ten times more adults than children get leukemia, it is the most common form of cancer in children. Until the second half of the twentieth century, having leukemia meant a virtual death sentence. Since then, scientists have developed better treatments for leukemia, such as chemotherapy (strong medications that kill cancer cells) and stem cell transplants (giving patients special kinds of cells that grow and divide into new blood cells). Currently, about 90 percent of children under five years old with certain forms of leukemia survive. Nearly one-quarter of a million Americans are living with leukemia or are in remission.

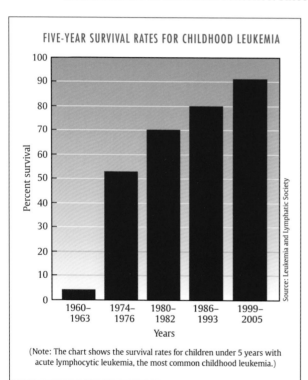

FIVE-YEAR SURVIVAL RATES FOR CHILDHOOD LEUKEMIA

Percent survival

Years

Source: Leukemia and Lymphatic Society

(Note: The chart shows the survival rates for children under 5 years with acute lymphocytic leukemia, the most common childhood leukemia.)

Remission means that there is a decrease or disappearance of symptoms even though leukemia may still be present.

Meet Shannon, Dominic, Julian, Jake, Yvonne, Montana, Michael, and Aubrey. Leukemia affected all of their lives and the lives of their family and friends as well.

Eleven-year-old Shannon Tavaraz had the thrill of her life when she scored a leading role in the Broadway musical The Lion King. *For months Shannon played Young Nala four times a week in the show. Then she got backaches and a runny nose. At first her doctor thought she had a cold. Instead, blood tests showed the young starlet had leukemia.*

When Dominic Mott was five years old, he spent Christmas Eve in the emergency room with a high fever. Then every couple of weeks, the fever returned. Doctors discovered after several months that the little boy had leukemia. They began a two-year treatment program that seemed to work. It looked as if Dominic would be able to start kindergarten.

Fourteen-year-old Julian McCann's parents thought he had swine flu when he came down with a fever. But he was sick for three weeks, longer than flu usually lasts. A blood test showed he had leukemia. Julian had a tough course of chemotherapy that didn't help very much. Doctors said Julian needed a stem cell transplant.

Fifteen-year-old Jake Owen collided with another boy during a baseball game. The other boy jumped right up, but Jake went to the dugout to lie down on the bench. The coach called Jake's mom to the dugout and told her that Jake needed to see a doctor. The doctor found that Jake was bleeding internally from a swollen spleen due to leukemia.

Dan Schmidt took his new wife, Yvonne, to the doctor the day after they got married. Yvonne hadn't felt well for weeks but chalked it up to the stress of planning a big wedding. After several hours of examinations and tests, the doctor told Yvonne and Dan that she had leukemia. Their honeymoon would have to wait.

November 11, 2009

From the Pages of USA TODAY

Abdul-Jabbar's leukemia rare but treatable

The news that basketball Hall of Famer Kareem Abdul-Jabbar, the NBA's all-time leading scorer, has a rare but treatable form of leukemia hit fellow UCLA alum Bill Walton hard. "When the story came over the wire in the middle of the night, I couldn't sleep at all," said Walton, who followed in Abdul-Jabbar's footsteps as a center for the UCLA basketball program. "Kareem is a hero to us all."

The good news is that Abdul-Jabbar's prognosis is promising. Diagnosed with chronic myeloid leukemia, Abdul-Jabbar, 62, said doctors told him he can manage and live with this condition. Normally private, he said he had no qualms about taking his health issue public.

"Early detection and treatment really are the keys for anyone who has to deal with this condition," he said. "I wanted to educate people about how modern medicine works. If I can help save some lives, I'm very happy to do that."

Abdul-Jabbar, a Lakers special assistant coach, was overwhelmed by the support shown. "He's the proudest of men, the most talented of men and the kindest of men," Walton said. "It's our duty, obligation and respect to do whatever we can to help him through this difficult time. He'll do what he's always done. He has always given people hope."

Abdul-Jabbar can maintain his regular lifestyle. He said, "I have to take the time to see my specialist. I have to go on a regular basis to have my blood analyzed, and I have to take my medication."

—*Jeff Zillgitt*

Basketball great Kareem Abdul-Jabbar, pictured here in 2004, was diagnosed with leukemia in 2008.

Montana Oatman was just two years old when his parents noticed that he was often too tired to play. They took him to two doctors who couldn't find anything wrong. The third doctor did a blood test and told Montana's parents he had leukemia. The doctor referred Montana to St. Jude Children's Research Hospital, a leading children's cancer center.

Michael Billig was forty-three years old and a popular anthropology professor at a Pennsylvania college when doctors told him that he had leukemia. After several rounds of grueling chemotherapy, he felt pretty good. But doctors said his leukemia was sure to return unless he tried a new type of stem cell transplant that might completely cure him.

Aubrey Williams was nine years old when her grandparents said she looked too pale. Aubrey's mother took her to the pediatrician to be checked out. The doctor sent Aubrey and her mother to a laboratory for a blood test. Five hours later, the doctor drove to Aubrey's house to tell her parents that Aubrey had leukemia.

This book will tell you about the different forms of leukemia, what they have in common, and how they differ. It will describe the symptoms of leukemia. You will learn about the challenges of living with leukemia and how doctors diagnose and treat it. And you will read about intriguing new research into the causes of leukemia. This research will surely lead to even better treatments and perhaps complete cures for more people. Read on to learn about leukemia, the disease of giant spleens and white blood.

USA TODAY

CHAPTER ONE

LEUKEMIA BASICS

During an open audition in 2009, Shannon Tavarez won the role of Young Nala in the Broadway show The Lion King. Shannon was just eleven years old, and it looked as though her career was off to a quick start. She juggled schoolwork as she performed four shows each week for several months. Then, in April 2010, things started to go terribly wrong. "My lower back and legs were tight and it hurt to walk," Shannon said. "It hit me really hard, like someone was throwing a ball at me." Cast members said she also had a runny nose and pasty-looking skin.

According to Shannon's mother, the family doctor thought she had a bad cold. When Shannon didn't get better, her mother took her to another doctor. A blood test showed that Shannon had a very serious form of leukemia called acute myeloid leukemia. Shannon had to leave The Lion King in April 2010. Doctors started her treatment right away. They injected chemotherapy into her spine to try to control the leukemia. Shannon spent much of her time in a children's hospital on Long Island, New York. She went through a second round of chemotherapy while she waited for a stem cell transplant.

Shannon Tavarez (right) and her mom, Odiney Brown, posed for a picture at a children's hospital in New York, where Shannon underwent treatment for leukemia.

As recently as 1960, doctors believed that leukemia was incurable and inevitably fatal. At that time, antibiotics could cure most infections. Surgeons could remove a bad appendix or gallbladder. A plaster cast allowed a broken arm to heal. But doctors had no idea what caused leukemia, much less how to cure it. Over the past fifty years, researchers have learned much about leukemia and made great strides in developing treatments. Even so, leukemia is a frightening and dangerous disease for patients and their families.

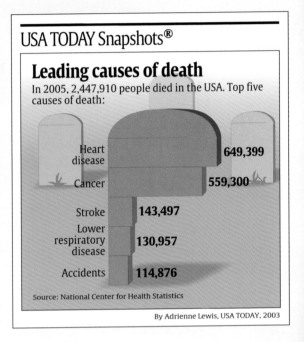

USA TODAY Snapshots®

Leading causes of death

In 2005, 2,447,910 people died in the USA. Top five causes of death:

Heart disease — 649,399

Cancer — 559,300

Stroke — 143,497

Lower respiratory disease — 130,957

Accidents — 114,876

Source: National Center for Health Statistics

By Adrienne Lewis, USA TODAY, 2003

WHO GETS LEUKEMIA?

In 2010 doctors diagnosed approximately 43,050 new cases of leukemia. That may seem like a lot, but about 207,000 women developed breast cancer that same year. An estimated 217,730 men developed prostate cancer, and 222,520 men and women developed lung cancer. Because leukemia is the most common childhood cancer, many people think of it as a childhood disease. But leukemia strikes ten times more adults than children. Most cases of leukemia occur in older adults. The average age of people who are newly diagnosed with leukemia is sixty-six years old.

MOST COMMON CHILDHOOD CANCERS

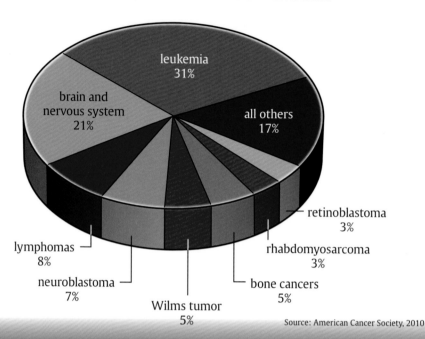

leukemia
31%

brain and
nervous system
21%

all others
17%

retinoblastoma
3%

lymphomas
8%

rhabdomyosarcoma
3%

neuroblastoma
7%

bone cancers
5%

Wilms tumor
5%

Source: American Cancer Society, 2010

This pie chart shows that leukemia is the most common cancer in children.

Leukemia is among the top fifteen frequently occurring cancers in all races. However, the incidence of leukemia varies considerably by ethnicity. Rates are highest among whites, followed by African Americans and Hispanics. Asian/Pacific Islanders and American Indian/ Alaskan Natives have the fewest cases of leukemia. And leukemia does not strike the genders equally. More males than females develop leukemia. About 57 percent of new cases of leukemia occur in boys and men, while 43 percent occur in girls and women.

More than 250,000 people in the United States are living with leukemia or are in remission (having no more symptoms). Advances in treatment have dramatically improved survival rates for most forms of the cancer. Depending on the type of leukemia and the age of the patient, five-year survival rates vary from 23 percent to over 90 percent. Leukemia is no longer the near-certain death sentence it once was. Many people with leukemia live normal or near-normal lives for many years. And an increasing number are completely cured.

LEUKEMIA RISK FACTORS

Scientists don't know for sure why one person develops leukemia and another one doesn't, but they have identified some risk factors. A risk factor is something that affects a person's chance of getting a disease, such as cancer. For example, smoking is a huge risk factor for lung cancer. Too much ultraviolet radiation from time spent in the sun or in a tanning booth is a risk factor for skin cancer. Known risk factors for leukemia include various types of radiation, exposure to chemicals, certain disorders, and a virus.

HIGH-ENERGY RADIATION

People exposed to high levels of radiation are much more likely to get leukemia than those without such exposure. For example, in 1945 the United States dropped two atomic bombs over Japan near the end of World War II (1939–1945). The bombs released large amounts of radiation. Many Japanese who were exposed to the radiation developed leukemia in the following years.

That was the first time—but not the last—that large amounts of radiation escaped into the environment. In 1959 atmospheric (above-Earth) hydrogen bomb tests in Siberia and over the Pacific Ocean were linked to an increased rate of leukemia, also in Japan. The massive amount of radiation that leaked when a nuclear reactor exploded in 1986 at Chernobyl in the Ukraine greatly increased the rate of leukemia and other cancers in that region of Eastern Europe.

The Chernobyl Disaster

Early in the morning of April 26, 1986, workers at a nuclear reactor at the Chernobyl power plant in northern Ukraine were testing the reactor's cooling system. The test failed due to mechanical and human errors. At 1:23 A.M., the reactor exploded, releasing one hundred times more radiation than did the atomic bombs dropped over Hiroshima and Nagasaki, Japan, in 1945. United Nations experts call the Chernobyl explosion the greatest industrial disaster in the history of humankind.

Most of the radiation was deposited in the countries of Belarus, Ukraine, and Russia. But winds sent radiation plumes over large parts of Europe as well. Radioactive materials included iodine, cesium, strontium, and plutonium. Plutonium has a half-life of 24,100 years. That means it will take that long for half of the plutonium atoms to decay into nonradioactive materials. Radiation remains in the soil, water, and the trees of the region. At an international meeting about Chernobyl in 2009, experts said some areas will remain uninhabitable for more than one thousand years.

The number of deaths resulting from Chernobyl remains controversial, with figures ranging from a few dozen to tens of thousands. In 2002 Ukraine reported that 84 percent of the three million people who had been exposed to the radiation were sick. One million of them are children. Thyroid cancer and leukemia are the most common radiation-related illnesses in the region. In one part of Belarus, clinics reported a 50 percent increase in leukemia among both adults and children. The Chernobyl radiation will affect people for decades to come.

In 1963 the United States and many other countries pledged to stop testing nuclear weapons in the atmosphere. Instead, they agreed to test such weapons underground to reduce the risk of releasing harmful radiation. France continued atmospheric testing until 1974, and China continued until 1980. Most countries have stopped testing nuclear weapons entirely. However, India and Pakistan performed underground testing in 1998. North Korea performed the last known underground nuclear testing in 2009. At least ten countries possess nuclear weapons, and many others use nuclear reactors to generate electricity. The potential for purposeful or accidental release of large amounts of radiation still exists. Japan faced a nuclear crisis in 2011 after a huge earthquake and tsunami damaged reactors at a nuclear power plant on its north coast.

MEDICAL RADIATION AND CHEMOTHERAPY

People treated for certain kinds of cancer with radiation therapy have a higher risk of later developing leukemia. People also receive radiation during routine dental and medical X-rays. Until 2010, researchers did not know if an average amount of medical radiation increased the risk for leukemia. A study published that year in the *International Journal of Epidemiology*, a scholarly journal that focuses on the incidence and spread of diseases, found that medical radiation did appear to increase the risk. The study looked at 827 children with leukemia who were less than fifteen years old. Results surprised even the experts. Children with the most common form of childhood leukemia had nearly twice the chance of having had three or more X-rays than children without leukemia. Researchers say more studies are needed. They suggest parents discuss the need for X-rays with their child's doctor to decide if the benefit outweighs the possible risk. Chemotherapy, used to treat cancer, may also increase the patient's risk for developing leukemia at a later time.

www.usatoday.com

USA TODAY

Life
SECTION D

August 4, 2005

From the Pages of USA TODAY

Hope floats on wings of a crane

Hiroshima victim's wish for peace continues to increase a thousandfold

The 60th anniversary of the bombing of Hiroshima will be commemorated with solemn words, silent prayers and countless brightly colored paper cranes.

The origami cranes pay tribute to one young victim of the atomic bomb, Sadako Sasaki, who has become an international symbol of all young victims of war. Ten million cranes are sent each year to Hiroshima's Peace Memorial Park. Long garlands of them are displayed before the Children's Peace Monument, which bears Sadako's image.

Sadako was a frightened 12-year-old girl with leukemia who began folding origami in the hope that the cranes would bring good luck. Sadako was 2 when the atomic bomb exploded a mile [1.6 kilometers] from her house in Hiroshima. A decade later, when she was dying of radiation-related leukemia, she heard an ancient legend that promised that anyone who made 1,000 cranes would be granted her dearest wish. Sadako crafted delicate origami birds from her hospital bed, using every scrap of paper she could find.

BENZENE AND OTHER CHEMICALS

Benzene is a chemical found in some industrial workplaces. For example, benzene can be found at company plants that manufacture drugs, plastics, dyes, and synthetic rubber. Gasoline and cigarette smoke both contain benzene. Crude oil also contains a lot of benzene. Some experts warn that the oil spill in the Gulf of Mexico in 2010 may prove hazardous in coming years to those who worked to clean up the beaches. Certain volatile solvents—liquid chemicals

A childhood friend, Ritsuko Komaki, says she is still touched by the way Sadako transformed these reminders of her illness into images of hope. As a child, Komaki says, she wondered why many who were exposed to fallout died, while others, such as her grandmother, recovered. She became a doctor to answer those questions and to help other leukemia patients. Komaki is a professor of radiation oncology at Houston's M.D. Anderson Cancer Center.

"When Sadako died, I could have been just sad and angry," Komaki says. "Instead of getting angry and making enemies, we have to make peace to make the bad things into better things. That's the way we can forgive each other." Komaki says she is encouraged that people haven't forgotten the victims of Hiroshima. "Sadako would be pleased if we could make this world a little more peaceful," Komaki says. "Her heart belonged to peace."

—Liz Szabo

Origami cranes have become an international symbol of peace since people around the world learned the story of Sadako Sasaki, a victim of radiation-related leukemia.

that evaporate into a gas form (such as paint thinner, formaldehyde, and chemicals used in dry cleaning)—are believed to increase the risk of leukemia as well.

PESTICIDES AND HERBICIDES

The use of certain chemicals to kill unwanted pests and weeds is believed to increase the risk for developing leukemia. Tens of thousands of U.S. veterans who served in the Vietnam War between 1964 and 1975 were exposed to the herbicide known as Agent Orange. Agent Orange was used to kill trees and brush in Vietnam's jungles to reduce hiding places for North Vietnamese soldiers. It allowed helicopter pilots to see the ground and find enemy soldiers. Veterans claimed for years that Agent Orange caused many diseases, including cancer. In 2009 the Department of Veterans Affairs added two types of leukemia to the list of diseases caused by Agent Orange.

DOWN SYNDROME AND MYELODYSPLASTIC SYNDROME

Down syndrome is an inherited genetic disorder. People with Down syndrome and several other rare inherited diseases have an increased chance of developing leukemia. Scientists have not yet discovered why this is true.

A serious blood disorder called myelodysplastic syndrome, sometimes known as pre-leukemia, increases the risk for developing leukemia. People with this disorder cannot make enough of certain blood cells. Doctors may be able to control the disorder in some patients, but others will go on to develop full-blown leukemia.

HUMAN T-CELL LEUKEMIA VIRUS TYPE 1 (HTLV-1)

This virus increases the risk for developing a rare type of leukemia called adult T-cell leukemia. Between 2 percent and 5 percent of people infected with the virus develop leukemia. The virus that causes the disease is not as contagious as many other viruses, such as the viruses that cause influenza and hepatitis. However, doctors believe HTLV-1 can be passed through sexual contact, use of dirty needles for injecting drugs, and from mother to breast-feeding infant. HTLV-1 is not the only virus that causes cancer. Viruses cause an estimated 15 percent of all cancers, such as some forms of liver cancer and cervical cancer.

FAMILY HISTORY

It's rare for more than one person in a family to have leukemia. When it does happen, it usually involves a form of chronic leukemia. The family connection for leukemia is most notable in identical twins. If one twin develops leukemia, the other twin has a 20 percent increased risk of developing it as well. Fraternal twins and non-twin siblings have only a slightly increased risk for developing leukemia if another sibling has it. A parent who developed leukemia as an adult does not appear to increase the risk for his or her children.

Having a risk factor does not mean that a person will get leukemia or any other kind of cancer. It only means that the chances are somewhat higher than someone without the same risk factor. In fact, most people who develop leukemia do not have any known risk factors. Others who have one or more risk factors never develop leukemia.

SHANNON'S BEST CHANCE

Doctors said that Shannon's best chance of recovering from the aggressive form of acute myeloid leukemia she had would be a stem cell transplant. Shannon's father was Hispanic and her mother is African American. Being of mixed race makes it more difficult to find a stem cell donor. Cast members of The Lion King *started a donor drive, as did singers Rihanna, Alicia Keys, and rapper 50 Cent. Hundreds of people volunteered to be tested to see if they could donate to Shannon or others in need. In August 2010, Shannon underwent a stem cell transplant from matched umbilical cord blood.*

CHAPTER TWO

BLOOD AND BONE MARROW

Dominic Mott didn't have a good Christmas Eve. The five-year-old spent that day in the emergency room with a high fever. The fever came and went for weeks. A few months later, doctors diagnosed Dominic with acute lymphocytic leukemia. For nearly two years, he routinely received chemotherapy through a tube inserted into his vein (an intravenous, or IV, tube). Several months of oral chemotherapy (taken by mouth) followed. At first, it seemed that the medications were working, but Dominic's leukemia returned.

In February 2008, doctors gave Dominic's grandmother, Margie Mott, some bad news. They said he would need a bone marrow transplant within six months or he would not survive. "I can't describe the black hole," said his grandmother, who had raised Dominic since he was three years old. "We were told that with a perfect match, Dominic had a 20 percent chance of success. And then they said we weren't likely to find a perfect match because he's biracial." Dominic's mother is black, and his father is white—but less than 3 percent of people registered to be bone marrow donors are biracial.

While there are several types of leukemia, they all have something in common—an overproduction of abnormal blood cells in the bone marrow. The effects of leukemia and the symptoms that people experience are directly related to the type of blood cells involved. To understand leukemia, it is helpful to first know about blood and the different types of blood cells, how they work, and where they come from.

BLOOD AND BLOOD CELLS

A body tissue is a collection of similar cells that perform one or more specific functions. Most tissues are physically connected to one another, for example, the tissues that form skin and muscles. Blood is also a type of tissue—a liquid tissue. Blood contains different types of cells that are not physically connected to one another. These cells work together to carry out several tasks necessary to life. The heart pumps blood through every part of the body, reaching each cell through tiny vessels. Blood serves many functions:

- Transportation. Blood carries oxygen and nutrients to body cells. It carries carbon dioxide and other waste products from cells to the lungs and the kidneys, where they are removed from the body. Blood also transports important hormones, or chemicals that affect other parts of the body, from glands such as the thyroid and the pituitary. The pituitary is the "master gland" in the brain that directly or indirectly affects most bodily functions.
- Acid-base regulation. Blood controls certain substances to keep the body in ideal chemical balance. For example, one kind of acid breaks down to become carbon dioxide and water. The lungs exhale the carbon dioxide, and the kidneys excrete the water. This process keeps the body from becoming too acidic.
- Thermoregulation. Blood carries heat to the skin to cool the body off when it is too warm. Blood vessels constrict to hold in body heat when the temperature is cold.
- Immunity. Blood carries different types of white blood cells to injured tissues to help fight against infection. The white blood cells kill invading microbes such as bacteria and viruses. Some white blood cells can kill cancer cells as well.
- Hemostasis. Blood carries substances that work with platelets to help blood to clot when an injury damages a blood vessel.

Blood makes up about 7 percent of a person's total body weight. Women have about 4.5 liters (4.7 quarts) of blood, and men have about 5.5 liters (5.8 quarts). A little over half of the blood is plasma.

www.usatoday.com

Life
SECTION D

August 4, 2003

From the Pages of USA TODAY

Group is on a mission to sign up more black organ donors

Myths have held some back

A black women's organization launched an educational initiative in eleven U.S. cities to encourage more blacks to sign organ-donor cards. Linkages to Life, a partnership between not-for-profit The Links Inc. and Roche Pharmaceuticals, aims to educate African-American communities about organ donation and dispel myths that have long prevented many members of this minority group from signing a donation registry.

"We want to get the message to the mainstream," says Links president Gladys Vaughn. "This is not going to happen overnight. It's going to be a slow march, but we are willing to walk."

Of the sixteen people who die waiting for organ transplants each day in the USA, half of them are ethnic minorities, and a quarter of them are black. The chances of finding a perfect match for a black transplant recipient are greatly increased

Plasma is mostly made up of water, but it also contains other substances such as proteins, glucose (sugar), minerals (iron, calcium, potassium, and sodium), vitamins, and waste products.

The rest of the blood is made up of various kinds of blood cells: red blood cells, platelets, and white blood cells. All of these blood cells are formed in the bone marrow. Leukemia directly affects all of them.

RED BLOOD CELLS

The vast majority of blood cells are red blood cells. There are seven hundred times more red blood cells than white blood cells circulating if the donor is of the same ethnicity, experts say.

The rate of African-American organ donation has risen since the 1980s and is now commensurate with the nation's black population. But that is not enough, says Clive Callender, professor of surgery at Howard University in Washington, D.C. "African-Americans still donate less frequently than we'd like them to do, because they are in greater need," he says. Blacks are at higher risk for hypertension and diabetes, conditions that often lead to organ failure. Though they are 12% of the U.S. population, blacks make up 35% of the kidney transplant waiting list.

Callender cites many people's distrust of the nation's health care system and fear that having signed an organ-donor card would impede medical attention during an emergency. He says education is the most successful method of boosting the number of donors. "When the message is delivered by the appropriate minority person, people become part of the solution to the problem."

—*Claire Bourne*

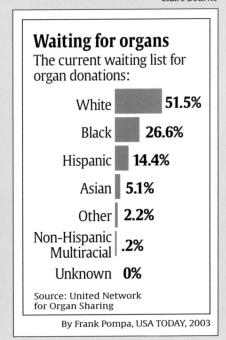

Waiting for organs

The current waiting list for organ donations:

White	51.5%
Black	26.6%
Hispanic	14.4%
Asian	5.1%
Other	2.2%
Non-Hispanic Multiracial	.2%
Unknown	0%

Source: United Network for Organ Sharing

By Frank Pompa, USA TODAY, 2003

in the bloodstream. This is why blood looks red. Each red blood cell, also called an erythrocyte, carries millions of hemoglobin molecules. (A molecule is the smallest complete unit of an element or a compound.) Each hemoglobin molecule carries four oxygen molecules. Red blood cells carry vital oxygen into every cell of the body. The redder the blood is, the more oxygen it contains. That's why arterial blood, which is filled with oxygen as it passes through blood vessels in the lungs, is bright red.

Venous blood—the blood returning from the body to the heart—is less red, even slightly blue-tinged. By the time venous blood reaches the heart, it has already released most of its oxygen to cells. The bone marrow continually makes new red blood cells because they only live for about four months. The spleen breaks down old red blood cells and recycles the hemoglobin.

People with leukemia don't have enough red blood cells to carry sufficient oxygen. This is one reason why leukemia patients are tired and have little energy.

PLATELETS

Platelets begin as giant cells called megakaryocytes produced in the bone marrow. The megakaryocyte breaks into the tiny particles called platelets (also known as thrombocytes). Platelets are not cells. Platelets are just fragments of the megakaryocytes. Platelets live between five and ten days. Normally, we don't run short of platelets because healthy bone marrow constantly makes new ones.

Platelets contain several substances involved in blood clotting. People with leukemia don't have enough platelets. That is why they bruise so easily and why they may bleed a lot from tiny cuts. Sometimes leukemia patients bleed from their gums when they brush their teeth.

WHITE BLOOD CELLS

The bone marrow makes two types of cells that change into a variety of white blood cells. White blood cells live from a few hours to a few weeks, depending on their type. Healthy bone marrow continually produces a new supply of these cells too.

One type of white blood cell releases a chemical called histamine that causes inflammation and allergic reactions as part of the immune response. (The body's immune system fights off invading viruses, bacteria, and other foreign substances.) Some white blood cells help to destroy parasites. Monocytes are white blood cells that turn into macrophages when they sense foreign substances such as viruses and bacteria. Macrophages can change their shape and squeeze between cells. They leave the bloodstream and enter body tissues to engulf and kill huge numbers of invading bacteria. Lymphocytes are a major class of white blood cells that specialize in killing bacteria and viruses. They do not squeeze between cells but largely remain in the bloodstream and lymph nodes.

White blood cells help to fight infection and heal wounds. But people with leukemia have far too many white blood cells. And most of those white blood cells are abnormal or too immature to fight infection. People with leukemia often get sick because they don't have enough healthy white blood cells to fight infection. The problem stems from deep within the bones. Red blood cells, platelets, and white blood cells: all of these amazing cells begin life inside our bone marrow.

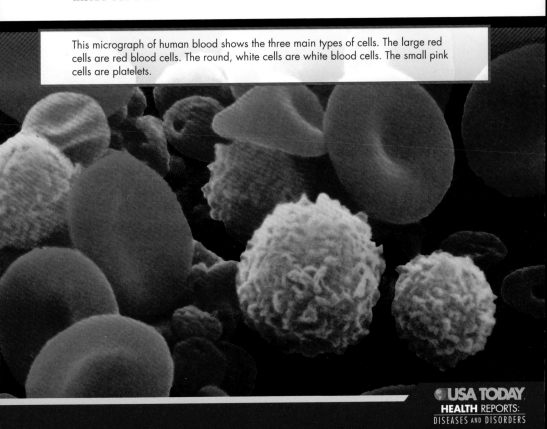

This micrograph of human blood shows the three main types of cells. The large red cells are red blood cells. The round, white cells are white blood cells. The small pink cells are platelets.

MEET YOUR MARROW

Bones are not just the hard, dead, pale objects that make up skeletons you may have seen on television or in a museum or a biology laboratory. Inside a human body, bones are living systems,

Red blood cells, platelets, and white blood cells all begin life in the bone marrow deep within our bones.

INSIDE BONE MARROW

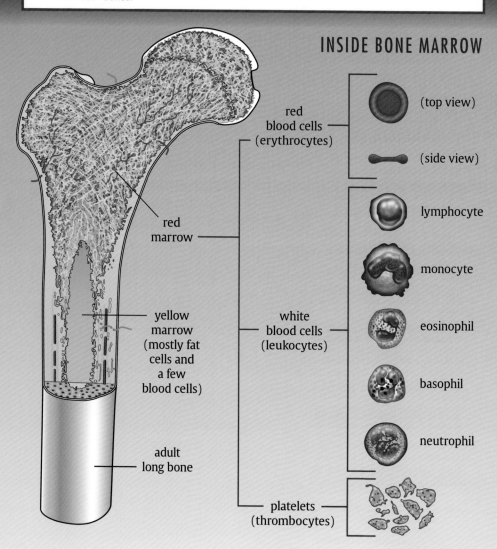

red blood cells (erythrocytes)
(top view)
(side view)

red marrow

yellow marrow (mostly fat cells and a few blood cells)

white blood cells (leukocytes)
lymphocyte
monocyte
eosinophil
basophil
neutrophil

adult long bone

platelets (thrombocytes)

continually repairing and renewing themselves. Minerals such as calcium and phosphorus, which the body takes from food and drinks, make bones hard. Tough connective fibers help hold bones together. And like all living tissues, bones have their own supply of nerves and blood vessels. Tiny arteries bring oxygen and nutrients into bones. Tiny veins carry waste products away.

Inside some of our bones is the soft, spongy material known as bone marrow. In children and teens, bone marrow is found inside the long bones, such as the femur (thigh bone), and the flat bones, such as the sternum (breastbone) and hip bones. In adults, bone marrow disappears from the leg bones. It is only found in the hip bones and sternum.

There are two types of bone marrow: yellow and red. Yellow marrow is made mostly of fat and serves as a form of stored energy. Red marrow produces the vital blood cells that our body needs.

All blood cells, no matter what kind, come from blood stem cells (sometimes called pluripotent or multipotent stem cells) located in

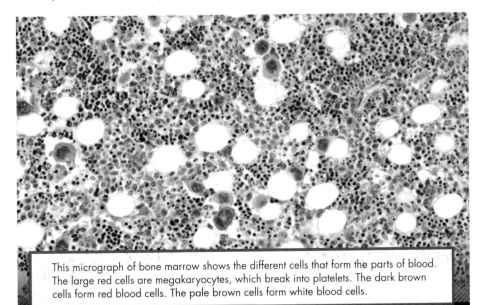

This micrograph of bone marrow shows the different cells that form the parts of blood. The large red cells are megakaryocytes, which break into platelets. The dark brown cells form red blood cells. The pale brown cells form white blood cells.

the red bone marrow. These stem cells are simple, self-renewing cells that are not yet specialized. It's as if these young cells haven't decided what they want to be when they grow up. A blood stem cell has the ability to form both myeloid stem cells and lymphoid stem cells. Think of myeloid stem cells and lymphoid stem cells as two branches of the blood stem cell family tree.

This diagram shows the many different substances that may develop from a blood stem cell.

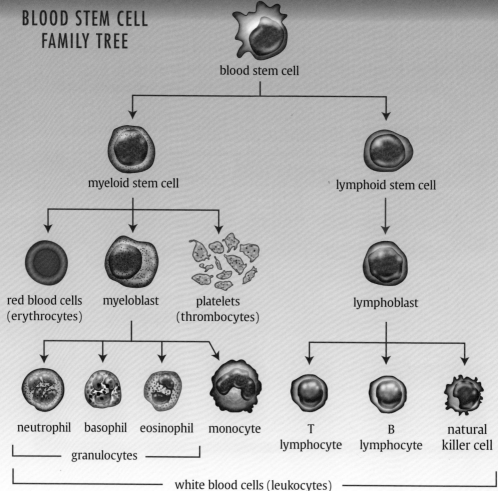

BLOOD STEM CELL FAMILY TREE

blood stem cell

myeloid stem cell

lymphoid stem cell

red blood cells (erythrocytes)

myeloblast

platelets (thrombocytes)

lymphoblast

neutrophil basophil eosinophil monocyte

T lymphocyte

B lymphocyte

natural killer cell

granulocytes

white blood cells (leukocytes)

What Do Blood Cells Do?

Blood Cells That Develop from Myeloid Stem Cells

Red blood cells: carry oxygen around the body via the bloodstream

Platelets: help with blood clotting

Myeloblasts are white blood cells that turn into several other types of white blood cells:

- Monocytes turn into macrophages and leave the bloodstream to enter body cells and fight infection.

- Eosinophils are involved with bodily response to inflammation, including allergies and asthma.

- Basophils are involved with inflammation and allergic reactions. They help to fight parasites.

- Neutrophils fight infection and inflammation. These cells make up the pus that occurs with infection.

Blood Cells That Develop from Lymphoid Stem Cells

Lymphoblasts turn into three kinds of white blood cells:

- B lymphocytes make antibodies to fight bacteria and viruses.

- T lymphocytes help to activate macrophages and natural killer cells. They release substances that directly kill invading cells.

- Natural killer cells bond to tumor and viral cells and release substances to kill them.

Still inside the marrow, the myeloid stem cells and the lymphoid stem cells undergo a series of changes as they mature. The myeloid stem cell produces red blood cells, platelets, and myeloblasts. The myeloblasts go on to develop into several types of white blood cells. Lymphoid stem cells become lymphoblasts, which in turn create the white blood cells known as lymphocytes and natural killer cells.

Bone marrow is like a nursery for blood cells. Normally, blood cells remain inside the bone marrow until they are mature. Blood passes through the bone marrow in tiny vessels and picks up the fully developed, mature blood cells and delivers them to the bloodstream. Once inside the circulatory system, each type of cell begins to do the job for which it was designed. Most of the lymphocytes take up residence in the lymphatic system.

THE LYMPHATIC SYSTEM

The lymphatic system is nearly a mirror image of the circulatory system—minus the heart. It is an important part of our immune system. The lymphatic system is made up of tiny pathways called lymph vessels that are located near blood vessels. It also includes lymph nodes, the spleen, tonsils, adenoids (tissue at the back of the nasal passage), and the thymus gland (a gland located in the chest). The clear fluid that circulates through the lymphatic vessels is called lymph.

Lymphatic vessels connect the lymph nodes. We have between five hundred and six hundred lymph nodes scattered throughout our bodies. Clusters of lymph nodes are found under the arms, in the groin, around the neck, and inside the chest and the abdomen. The nodes are shaped like beans or peas and range in size from a few millimeters (0.25 to 0.5 inches), to one or two centimeters (0.5 inches to 1 inch).

THE LYMPHATIC SYSTEM

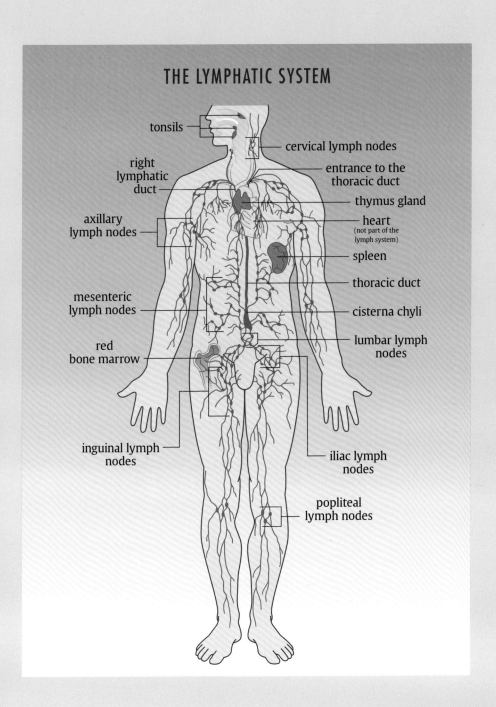

tonsils

cervical lymph nodes

right lymphatic duct

entrance to the thoracic duct

thymus gland

axillary lymph nodes

heart
(not part of the lymph system)

spleen

mesenteric lymph nodes

thoracic duct

cisterna chyli

red bone marrow

lumbar lymph nodes

inguinal lymph nodes

iliac lymph nodes

popliteal lymph nodes

Lymph nodes help to filter out microbes such as bacteria. For example, if you ever had strep throat, you might remember feeling swollen glands along the sides of your neck. Those swollen glands were actually lymph nodes doing their job of collecting the strep bacteria.

Once bacteria enter the lymph nodes, the white blood cells called lymphocytes start killing the bacteria. Nearly all the body's lymphocytes live within the lymphatic system. Only a small number remain in the circulating blood.

There are three types of lymphocytes. Leukemia may affect one or all of them:

- B lymphocytes make antibodies (proteins that help fight infection) in response to foreign antigens. Antigens are special protein markers on all cells that identify the cells as being either part of the body or coming from outside of the body. Microbes such as bacteria have antigen markers. The body's antibodies tag the invading microbes to identify them as foreign. This allows macrophages—white blood cells that can leave the blood circulation—to locate, surround, and digest the microbes.
- T lymphocytes protect the body against viruses and some cancer cells by producing chemicals to directly kill off the viruses.
- Natural killer cells (NK cells) kill antibody-tagged cells and cells infected with viruses and cancer.

Leukemia is a complex group of diseases that affects the bone marrow and white blood cells. Knowing a little bit about the different types of white blood cells makes it easier to understand leukemia and how it affects people. But what causes leukemia and how does it begin? Read on to learn about the causes of leukemia and the genetic changes that trigger it.

A DONOR FOR DOMINIC

Among seven potential stem-cell donors in Europe and the United States, none could provide a close enough match for Dominic. Meanwhile, less than 200 miles (320 km) from Dominic, in Bakersfield, California, a young man named Kevin Brewster went into the local blood bank to donate blood. He noticed a sign about bone marrow donation and was tested to be a donor. One month after being added to the donor registry, Brewster was called—he was a match for Dominic. Brewster said, "When you get a call saying you can save someone's life, you don't say no." Dominic received Brewster's bone marrow in a San Francisco hospital in July 2008.

CHAPTER THREE

IT'S ALL IN THE GENES

Julian McCann's family thought he had the swine flu when he developed a high fever. The fourteen-year-old was sick for three weeks. When Julian's parents took him to the doctor, blood tests showed he had acute lymphocytic leukemia. Instead of returning to his first year of high school and participating on the school's rifle team, he started several months of chemotherapy. It didn't work very well. His doctors said Julian needed a stem cell transplant.

Julian got lucky. His eleven-year-old brother, Seth, turned out to be the perfect match. "I'm saving his life," Seth said, "and he's kind of saving my life because I'm not being worried about him." Since the transplant, Julian has been cancer-free. He started his sophomore year of high school a few months later. But the expensive treatments cost far more than the family's insurance would pay. They still owed thousands and thousands of dollars in medical bills.

While science has identified several risk factors for developing leukemia, the actual cause of leukemia is genetic mutation. Genes are tiny segments of DNA, the genetic blueprint that makes every organism what it is. Our DNA determines how tall or short we are, if we have brown eyes or blue, and if we have black hair or blond. Mutations are permanent changes to DNA. Some genetic mutations are harmless. Others are harmful. Too much exposure to radiation or chemicals such as benzene may damage DNA, as can becoming infected with the HTLV-1 virus. These genetic mutations may lead to leukemia.

Often, however, a genetic mutation happens for no apparent reason. Most cancers—including leukemia—start with just one genetically damaged cell. That one cell then makes millions and billions of identical copies or clones of itself. It is this ability of a damaged cell to keep cloning itself that allows cancer to grow and spread. The sheer volume of abnormal cells overwhelms the body's immune system.

Genetic mutations in the myeloblasts or the lymphoblasts cause most forms of leukemia. The genetically damaged myeloblasts and lymphoblasts produce enormous quantities of abnormal, immature, and damaged white blood cells. Over time, the abnormal cells crowd out normal cells. There is simply not enough room for red blood cells or platelets. And there are not enough healthy white blood cells. Without treatment to reduce or eliminate abnormal blood cells, leukemia can be fatal.

BUSY CELLS

The cell is the basic structure of all living things. Bacteria are one-celled organisms. But it takes an estimated fifty to one hundred trillion cells to make up large, complex organisms such as humans. The human body contains over two hundred different types of cells. Cells group together to form organs, such as the liver, the heart, and the brain. Cells form tissues such as muscle and blood. Each type of cell is different. Scientists can identify which cells come from which organs or tissues when they view the cells under a microscope.

Cells divide rapidly during the early years of life as a child grows taller and bigger. This rapid growth and division of cells slows dramatically in adulthood when people reach their full size. Yet every human body must make new cells when old ones wear out or when injury or illness damages the organs and the tissues. A broken bone grows together again. A finger sliced by a knife heals itself.

September 14, 2009

From the Pages of USA TODAY

Leukemia, stem cell scientists get Laskers

One of the most prestigious prizes in medicine is being awarded this year to scientists working on stem cells and leukemia. The Lasker Awards, which are announced today, have been given since 1945. They recognize the contributions of scientists and physicians working to cure, treat and prevent disease.

"It's right up there with the Nobel Prize," says Gary Sieck, a research director at the Mayo Clinic, in Rochester, Minnesota. "The people who get it are at the top."

The Lasker-DeBakey Clinical Medical Research Award goes to three scientists whose work turned a fatal cancer, myeloid leukemia, into a manageable condition with their discovery of the drug Gleevec.

Brian Druker, 54, of Oregon Health & Science University, Nicholas Lydon, 52,

formerly of the Novartis pharmaceutical company, and Charles Sawyers, 50, of Memorial Sloan-Kettering Cancer Center did the work in the 1990s. The drug inhibits the protein made by an abnormal gene that causes this form of leukemia. Being awarded the prize is "an incredible badge of respect and honor," Sawyers says.

The Lasker Basic Medical Research Award goes to John Gurdon, 76, of Cambridge University and Shinya Yamanaka, 47, of Kyoto University. Their work has helped pave the way for the possibility of made-to-order stem cell treatments for individual patients.

The Lasker Awards are sometimes called "America's Nobels," in part because 76 Lasker laureates have gone on to receive the Nobel Prize.

—Elizabeth Weise

Cellular renewal is a constant process that maintains tissues and organs in a healthy and functional state. Cells grow and split in half to make new cells. As a cell prepares to split in half, it must first copy its DNA so that the new cell has an exact duplicate of the DNA in the old cell. Mistakes happen during this process. The mistakes may result in damage to the genes.

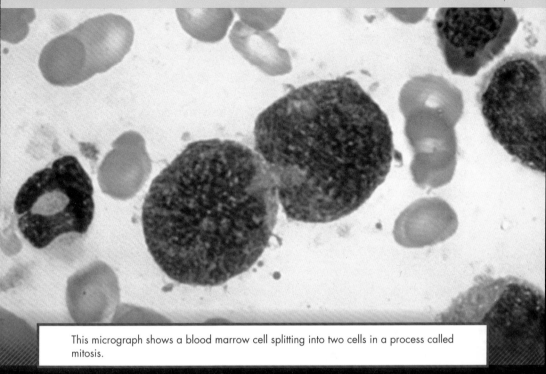

This micrograph shows a blood marrow cell splitting into two cells in a process called mitosis.

TO SPLIT OR NOT TO SPLIT?

Cells contain genes called tumor suppressor genes. These genes help to slow down cell division. They may delay a cell's division until the cell has time to repair its damaged DNA. If a cell is too damaged to repair itself, the tumor suppressor genes trigger apoptosis. Apoptosis is the self-destruction of damaged or sick cells. It's the deliberate suicide of an abnormal cell. Apoptosis is an important protective mechanism because it stops damaged or mutated genes from being passed on to a new generation of cells.

Cells also contain genes called proto-oncogenes. These genes help promote and regulate normal cell division. Proto-oncogenes tell cells, "It's time to split." Tumor suppressor genes say, "Hey, hold on a minute." Normally, proto-oncogenes and tumor suppressor genes work together to control cellular division. This means that the body produces just the right number of healthy new cells at just the right time.

Mutation or damage to either of these types of genes may cause leukemia and other kinds of cancer. If proto-oncogenes are genetically damaged, they can turn into oncogenes. Oncogenes actually promote the reproduction of defective and possibly cancerous cells. The oncogenes are stuck in high gear, sending out chemical signals that tell cells to keep on splitting, no matter what. Alternatively, when tumor suppressor genes are damaged, they can no longer put the brakes on abnormal cellular division. They can no longer trigger apoptosis or cellular suicide. The damaged cells keep on dividing.

TRANSLOCATING CHROMOSOMES

Abnormal chromosomes are another cause of leukemia. Chromosomes are structures within each cell that are made of coiled strands of DNA. The strands contain proteins and genes which are made up of smaller units of DNA. (Think about it this way: DNA is like a bunch of letters. Genes are like words. Chromosomes are like books.) Human cells (other than eggs and sperm) contain twenty-three pairs of chromosomes—one set from each parent. During cellular reproduction, chromosomes split and recombine to form duplicate sets of chromosomes in each new cell. Sometimes genes end up in the wrong place on the new chromosome. Scientists call this process translocation.

An abnormal chromosome called the Philadelphia chromosome is found in nearly all patients who have the form of leukemia called chronic myeloid leukemia. (The chromosome is named for the city in which it was discovered.) Because the translocation occurs in the myeloid stem cells within the bone marrow, the Philadelphia chromosome is found in all blood cells produced by the abnormal myeloid stem cells. The Philadelphia chromosome is also found in a few patients with other forms of leukemia. When it's present in leukemia other than chronic myeloid leukemia, it signals a poor prognosis (outcome).

The Philadelphia chromosome is not the only abnormal chromosome linked to leukemia. Scientists have identified about two hundred chromosomal abnormalities associated with leukemia and other cancers.

Other chromosome problems occur as cells prepare to divide. Deletions occur when part of a chromosome is lost. If the deletion involves, say, a tumor suppressor gene, the new cell may not function properly. Inversions occur when part of the chromosome gets turned around so it is in reverse order—sort of like a mirror image. This means the cell can no longer read its own genetic instructions. It is like trying to read a book held up to a mirror. An addition means the cell has an extra chromosome or part of one. In this case, too many copies of certain genes get into the new cell. If the extra genes are proto-oncogenes, the new cell may become cancerous.

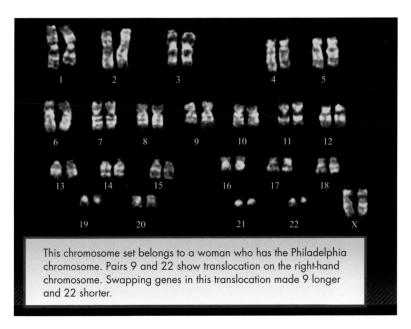

This chromosome set belongs to a woman who has the Philadelphia chromosome. Pairs 9 and 22 show translocation on the right-hand chromosome. Swapping genes in this translocation made 9 longer and 22 shorter.

National Cancer Registries

Hospitals and doctors around the nation report cancer statistics to state cancer registries. The states work with the Centers for Disease Control and Prevention to collect and analyze data about cancer cases and deaths. Reported cancers include leukemia; melanoma; and cancers of the breast, colon, liver, lung, and prostate.

Cancer registries help to monitor cancer trends over time and to determine cancer patterns in various populations (by age, gender, ethnicity, and state of residence). The registries help to guide planning and evaluation of cancer programs and to advance medical research.

LEUKEMIA STEM CELLS

Scientists have also discovered that some forms of leukemia are caused by leukemia stem cells. These are stem cells in the bone marrow that don't go on to become myeloid stem cells or lymphoid stem cells as they should. Leukemia stem cells are essentially immortal, duplicating themselves over and over again with nothing to stop them. Traditional treatments kill only the cancer cells that come from leukemia stem cells. As researchers learn more about leukemia stem cells, they hope to develop new ways to combat leukemia at its very source.

STANDING BY JULIAN

Julian's school and the small town where he lives near Buffalo, New York, were very supportive. The community sponsored a benefit to raise

money to help Julian's parents pay his medical bills.
The local Police Club did
the same. And members
of Julian's rifle club put on
a "Bald for Bucks" day at
the high school. Over two
dozen students and teach-
ers completely shaved
their heads for the event
to show support for Julian,
who lost his hair while on
chemotherapy. "This re-
ally struck us hard," said
Andrew Baumgartner, a
fellow rifle team member.
"We wanted to do some-
thing to show Julian that
we support him."

Julian McCann attends the Bald for Bucks fund-raiser thrown by his fellow rifle club members in 2010.

CHAPTER FOUR

SYMPTOMS AND DIAGNOSIS OF LEUKEMIA

I t turned out to be a lucky accident that fifteen-year-old Jake Owen crashed into another boy during a Texas baseball game. "I thought I was fine," Jake said. "I thought it was just the wind knocked out of me. Coach asked if I could still play, and I said yes. But then I started to move and couldn't do it. I went to the dugout and lay down on the bench." Jake's mom drove him to the hospital, where doctors said he was bleeding internally from his spleen. This sort of injury is not unusual in auto accidents or sports.

A surgeon removed Jake's spleen to stop the bleeding. But something else was going on. Blood tests showed that Jake had a large number of abnormal white blood cells. Further tests showed that he had chronic myeloid leukemia. "With this kind of leukemia, it's definitely better to pick it up in its early stages," said Dr. Robert Collins at the University of Texas Medical Center. Jake's mother was thankful. "It's just a freak thing that Jake got hurt," she said, "and that they found the leukemia so early."

The onset of leukemia can be acute or chronic. When people develop acute leukemia, they get sick quite suddenly, often in only a few weeks. Immature leukemia cells quickly reach an extremely high number. The cancerous white blood cells can't do the jobs that white blood cells are supposed to do. The symptoms of acute leukemia usually send people to their doctors because they feel very sick. Without treatment, a person may die of acute leukemia within a few months. But some forms of acute leukemia respond well to treatment, and people may be completely cured.

Chronic leukemia progresses slowly over many months or even years. Doctors often discover chronic leukemia during a routine medical checkup before the patient notices any symptoms. The doctor may order lab work, which usually includes an examination of blood cells under a microscope. The lab technician examining the cells may notice a very large number of white blood cells or that the cells are damaged or immature. People may live for years after being diagnosed with chronic leukemia. However, chronic leukemia is generally more difficult to treat and to cure than acute leukemia.

LEUKEMIA SYMPTOMS

Leukemia symptoms can be so mild that people may not realize that something is seriously wrong with them at first. Early symptoms of leukemia can be similar to those of the common cold, influenza, mononucleosis, and other illnesses. Sometimes leukemia is discovered by accident when a patient goes to his doctor for another problem or for a routine checkup. Other times, the symptoms come on so fast that a patient sees a doctor right away.

Some types of leukemia don't show symptoms for a long time. Doctors often discover them while doing routine screenings for other things.

Leukemia symptoms depend on how many of the body's white blood cells are affected and unable to do their work. The symptoms are much the same whether the patient has acute or chronic leukemia. What varies is how fast the symptoms come on and how intense they are. Symptoms of leukemia include the following:

- Pale skin (due to anemia—a shortage of oxygen-carrying red blood cells)
- Fatigue and weakness (due to anemia and infections)
- Infections and fever (due to a lack of normal white blood cells to help fight off bacteria and viruses; also leukemia cells may release harmful chemicals that cause fever)
- Swollen lymph nodes, especially in the neck or the armpit (leukemia cells may spread to lymph nodes and collect in them)
- Easy bruising or bleeding; frequent nosebleeds or bleeding from the gums and from small cuts (due to not enough platelets for the blood to properly clot)
- Swelling or pain in the abdomen from an enlarged spleen or liver (due to a collection of leukemia cells in those organs)
- Weight loss (due to poor appetite or a swollen spleen or liver pressing on the stomach making it difficult to eat)
- Pain in the bones and joints, especially in children (due to a buildup of leukemia cells in the bones and joints)
- Rashes (due to a collection of leukemia cells in the skin)
- Coughing or trouble breathing (due to the enlarged thymus gland in the chest pressing on the trachea or the windpipe in one type of leukemia)
- Swelling of face and arms (also due to enlargement of the thymus gland, which causes blood to back up in the veins)
- Headaches, vomiting, seizures, and vision problems, especially in children (due to leukemia cells entering the brain and the spinal fluid)

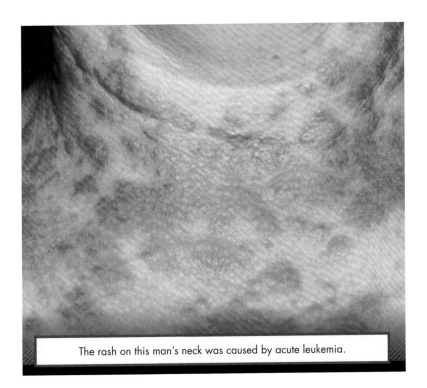

The rash on this man's neck was caused by acute leukemia.

- Pain, swelling, and malfunction of testicles, ovaries, kidneys, lungs, the heart, and other organs (due to leukemia cells entering those organs)

DIAGNOSING LEUKEMIA

Most of these symptoms can signal a number of other illnesses or cancers as well as leukemia. But once a doctor suspects leukemia, it is relatively easy to diagnose. It's very important to find out as soon as possible if a person has leukemia or another illness. Some forms of acute leukemia require immediate treatment, usually within days, if the patient is to survive. And it's vital to discover which type of white blood cells are affected—the myeloid or the lymphoid cells—because treatments may be different.

PHYSICAL EXAMINATION AND HISTORY

A doctor always starts by examining the patient and taking a medical history. The doctor listens to the heart and the lungs. She looks for bruises and feels for swollen lymph nodes. She asks about the current illness. How long has the patient felt sick, and what are the symptoms? And what in particular made the patient decide to seek medical care at this point? The doctor can see that the patient is sick, but she cannot be sure what is wrong without tests.

BLOOD TESTS

The first test for leukemia is a simple test called a complete blood count (CBC). A phlebotomist (a person who draws blood) or a medical assistant takes a sample of blood from a vein, usually in the arm. The CBC tells the doctor how many red blood cells and platelets are present. It also shows the number and type of white blood cells and how much oxygen-carrying hemoglobin the blood has.

The blood tests of patients with leukemia often show a lower than expected number of red blood cells and platelets. In chronic leukemia, the number of white blood cells is always high. With acute leukemia, white blood cell numbers may be very high, may be lower than normal, or the cells may be immature and unable to function normally. Four types of white blood cells come from the myeloid stem cells: monocytes, basophils, neutrophils, and eosinophils. Lymphoid stem cells produce the white blood cells called lymphocytes. The CBC shows how many of each kind are present, and if they are normal in size and appearance.

Family doctors and pediatricians generally do not perform the more specialized tests necessary to diagnose leukemia. If a patient has highly abnormal CBC results and the doctor suspects that the patient has leukemia, he will send that patient to a specialist. These specialists are oncologists (doctors who specialize in tumors) or hematologists (doctors who specialize in blood disorders such as leukemia).

BONE MARROW TESTS

If the CBC suggests leukemia, the specialist must test the bone marrow. This is the only way to find out exactly what is going on inside the bone marrow, where all blood cells are created and nurtured. The doctor usually takes a sample of bone marrow from the hip bone. Occasionally, bone marrow is drawn from the sternum instead. Patients may curl up on their sides or lie flat on their chests for the procedure.

If the patient is a child, the doctor will usually put the child to sleep with anesthesia. Once the child is sleeping, the doctor numbs the area where the needle goes in with a medication similar to what a dentist uses when filling a cavity. Adults are generally awake during a bone marrow test. Of course, they still receive the local numbing injection before the procedure.

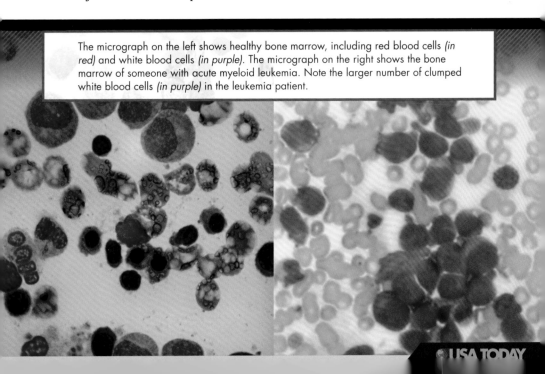

The micrograph on the left shows healthy bone marrow, including red blood cells *(in red)* and white blood cells *(in purple)*. The micrograph on the right shows the bone marrow of someone with acute myeloid leukemia. Note the larger number of clumped white blood cells *(in purple)* in the leukemia patient.

© USA TODAY

May 21, 2002

From the Pages of USA TODAY

Erasing signs of leukemia

Drug promising, but it may not help all patients

On Nov. 8, 2000, George Darr got news that would turn his life upside down. A routine blood test revealed that the Portland, Oregon resident had chronic myeloid leukemia (CML). He soon realized that the crushing fatigue he had written off to his killer work schedule was a symptom of the cancer.

Darr signed up for a study of a new drug called Gleevec. Three weeks after he started taking the drug, the white blood cells in Darr's bloodstream stopped multiplying like mad, and his energy level soared.

"I was incredibly lucky," he says about Gleevec, a drug that oncologists consider a revolutionary treatment for CML, a disease that strikes 5,000 people in the USA each year. Lead researcher Brian Druker of the Oregon Health & Science University

First, the doctor inserts a long, thin, hollow needle into the bone. He uses a syringe to draw out about a teaspoon (five milliliters) of fluid and cells from within the bone marrow. This is called the bone marrow aspiration. The marrow will be tested for problems in the cells or fluid. The doctor next performs the bone marrow biopsy using a larger hollow needle. He twists the needle and pushes downward until the needle enters the bone. He then pulls out the needle with a small sample of both bone and bone marrow. A doctor will examine this under a microscope to look for cancer cells and other problems. Both tests are needed so the doctor can determine what kind of unveiled findings from a new study of Gleevec during the annual meeting of the American Society of Clinical Oncology.

The findings suggest the drug erases many signs of the leukemia when given to people with an early form of the disease. The new findings add to previous reports of Gleevec's prowess. Researchers already had shown this drug could slow the progression of a very advanced form of CML, a disease that causes an explosion of white cells in the blood and bone marrow.

Druker wondered how well the drug would perform when given to people with an early form of the disease. He recruited over 1,000 people who had just gotten a diagnosis. Half the patients got Gleevec; the rest got the standard drug therapy of interferon. After a year, the team found that just 4% of people taking Gleevec had cancer that had gotten worse. In contrast, 19% of the interferon patients had cancer that had progressed.

Scientists who study this leukemia know that cancer cells can vanish from the bloodstream yet still lurk in the bone marrow. So Druker looked at bone marrow samples. They could find no evidence of leukemic cells in 68% of the people taking Gleevec. Just 7% of people taking interferon got the same good news.

Gleevec is one of the first drugs to target a specific defect that causes cancer. Unlike chemotherapy, which kills many cells in the body, even those that are not cancerous, Gleevec zeroes in on the leukemic cell. It works by blocking the action of an enzyme that cancer cells use to divide furiously. Without the enzyme action, the leukemic cell can't divide and eventually dies, Druker says.

—Kathleen Fackelmann

leukemia a person has and how it responds to treatment.

Most patients with leukemia will have one or more bone marrow tests during the course of treatment. The first sample tells the doctor what kind of leukemia the patient has and what percentage of the white blood cells are abnormal. The doctor may require additional bone marrow tests later to see how the patient responds to treatment. Does the bone marrow look normal, or is it still filled with abnormal cells? Although bone marrow tests cause soreness at the puncture site for a couple of days, they are necessary to be sure the treatment is working as it should.

USA TODAY

SPINAL TAP

The brain and the spinal cord make up the central nervous system. A fluid called the cerebrospinal fluid (CSF) surrounds the brain. CSF circulates through and around the brain and down into the spinal canal along the spinal cord. CSF helps to cushion and protect the brain and the spinal cord from injury.

In addition to the bone marrow tests, doctors often perform a spinal tap (or a lumbar puncture). In this test, the patient curls up on his or her side in the fetal position. This helps to separate the vertebra in the spine so that the doctor can insert a needle into the spinal canal between the bones. During a spinal tap, the doctor numbs the area with a local anesthetic and inserts the needle. She withdraws a small amount of fluid and sends it to the laboratory for examination.

There are two reasons why the doctor may perform a spinal tap. First, a spinal tap can determine if leukemia cells have left the blood and entered the central nervous system. If leukemia cells reach the central nervous system, the patient may experience headaches, vomiting, seizures, and problems with vision. Leukemia cells

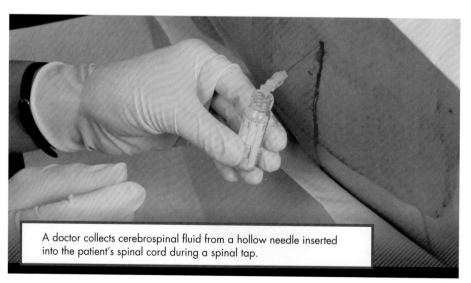

A doctor collects cerebrospinal fluid from a hollow needle inserted into the patient's spinal cord during a spinal tap.

normally don't get into the brain, nor do bacteria, viruses, or most medications. The brain has a powerful protective system called the blood-brain barrier. The blood-brain barrier keeps many organisms and substances from reaching the central nervous system.

But sometimes leukemia cells manage to breach the blood-brain barrier and collect on the surface of the brain and along the spinal cord. If the spinal tap shows that leukemia cells are in the CSF, it means they are collecting in clumps that put pressure on the brain and the spinal cord.

The second reason doctors must perform spinal taps on some leukemia patients is so they can inject medication directly into the CSF. This is the only way the medication can reach the leukemia cells in the central nervous system. Most medications that are swallowed or given into a vein do not reach the brain or the spinal cord. The blood-brain barrier keeps them out.

IMAGING STUDIES

Imaging studies include tests such as X-rays, computed tomography scans, magnetic resonance imaging (MRI) scans, and ultrasounds. Because leukemia does not cause tumors, imaging studies are not often needed. However, leukemia cells reproduce quickly and don't die when they should. The cancerous cells spill out of the bone marrow into the bloodstream, and they may gather in organs such as the spleen, the liver, the brain, or the spinal cord. If leukemia cells enter these organs, the organs cannot work correctly. Imaging studies are necessary if the doctor suspects that leukemia cells have spread in this manner.

Doctors use several imaging methods to study different areas or tissues of the body. CT scans are a specialized type of X-ray that produce detailed, cross-sectional images of the body. MRI scans use radio waves and magnets instead of X-rays. They are especially helpful for getting a good look at the brain and the spinal cord. Ultrasound examinations use sound waves to examine an internal organ. The sound waves produce an echo when they hit an organ. A computer converts the echoes into an image that shows on a screen. An ultrasound is useful to see if leukemia has caused abdominal organs such as the liver, the kidneys, and the spleen to become enlarged.

SPECIALIZED LABORATORY TESTS

Laboratories use specialized techniques to test samples of blood, bone marrow, and CSF. For example, certain dyes that only react with leukemia cells are used in a test called cytochemistry. Another test called flow cytometry can measure the amount of DNA in leukemia cells. It detects some forms of leukemia that are associated with a larger than normal amount of DNA in a cell. A test with the unusual nickname of FISH uses special dyes that attach to parts of chromosomes. This test can detect chromosome translocations, such as the Philadelphia chromosome, that are found in certain types of leukemia. A number of additional genetic tests may be required to confirm the diagnosis.

It is vital for doctors to know as much as possible about the type of leukemia that a patient has. Leukemia is not just classified as being acute or chronic. Doctors also must know if it comes from myeloid or lymphoid stem cells. They must know how mature or immature the leukemia cells are. Doctors require even more information about the DNA and the chromosomes found in any particular patient with leukemia. Once doctors know everything possible about a patient's leukemia, they can begin to plan treatment and predict the patient's outcome.

GETTING BACK IN THE GAME

In just a few weeks, Jake was back at the baseball field—although he wasn't yet playing. The surgery to remove Jake's enlarged spleen left an

Diagnosis by Dog?

Dogs have a great sense of smell. They can find people lost in the woods. Dogs can detect traces of explosives or drugs in airport luggage. They can locate people buried under earthquake rubble.

Dogs can be trained to help people with certain medical conditions too. They can smell the dangerously low blood sugar of a person with diabetes. They can smell the chemical changes that come before an epileptic seizure.

Doctors are discovering that dogs can be trained to smell cancer, as well. Cancers produce chemicals. In lab tests, dogs have correctly identified people with cancer of the bladder, the breast, and the prostate by smelling their urine. Dogs have found lung cancer by smelling a patient's breath. Two studies published in the medical journal *Lancet* showed that dogs could smell the difference between an ordinary mole and skin cancer.

Maybe one day, doctors can train dogs to sniff out leukemia as well. Perhaps all the abnormal white blood cells that go along with leukemia produce an odor that only a dog can detect. Imagine a doctor asking a collie for a consult!

8-inch (20-centimeter) scar on his abdomen. He needed a few more weeks of recovery time before he could play ball again. Jake takes five pills each morning to control his leukemia. One of the pills is called Gleevec. "Ten years ago a highly toxic bone marrow transplant was the typical treatment for patients with chronic myeloid leukemia," Dr. Collins said. "Gleevec changed everything. In treating CML, this medicine is a grand slam home run."

CHAPTER FIVE

TYPES OF LEUKEMIA

During wedding ceremonies, couples vow to stick together in sickness and in health. For Dan and Yvonne Schmidt, that vow was tested the day after their wedding. Before heading off on their honeymoon the next day, Dan took his new bride to the doctor. She had a bad sore throat that just wouldn't go away. After a quick blood test, the doctor sent the couple to a hospital for further tests to find out why her platelet count was dangerously low. Bruises also covered her body, and she felt light-headed even after removing her wedding tiara.

It didn't take long for doctors to find the answer. Yvonne had a rare type of leukemia called acute promyelocytic leukemia. The honeymoon would have to wait, because the treatment couldn't. Yvonne hadn't felt very well for weeks. "I just kept telling myself, it's the stress of the wedding," she said. "When we heard the news it was really hard to believe. I kept thinking, is there something I could have done? Why was this happening now?" Yvonne and Dan spent the first month of their marriage in a hospital room.

Doctors think about leukemia in two ways. First, they describe leukemia as being acute or chronic. Second, doctors classify leukemia by whether it starts in the myeloid stem cells or the lymphoid stem cells. Doctors may call the same type of leukemia by several names. For consistency, this book will use the terms that the American Cancer Society uses to describe the four major types of leukemia. These are the names and abbreviations you will read about in this chapter and the next:

- *Acute lymphocytic leukemia*—abbreviated as ALL (also called acute lymphoblastic leukemia or acute lymphoid leukemia)

- *Acute myeloid leukemia*—abbreviated as AML (also called acute myelogenous leukemia, or acute myelocytic leukemia)
- *Chronic lymphocytic leukemia*—abbreviated as CLL (also called chronic lymphoblastic leukemia, or chronic lymphoid leukemia)
- *Chronic myeloid leukemia*—abbreviated as CML (also called chronic myelogenous leukemia, or chronic myelocytic leukemia)

ACUTE LYMPHOCYTIC LEUKEMIA

Acute lymphocytic leukemia is a fairly rare cancer. It accounts for about 2 percent of all cancers in the United States. A person's lifetime risk of developing ALL is about one in one thousand. If that seems high, consider this: One out of eight American women will develop breast cancer in her lifetime. One out of six American men will develop prostate cancer.

ALL is more common in men than in women and more common in whites than in African Americans. ALL also occurs more often in people of higher socioeconomic status and among citizens of developed nations. Some scientists have a hypothesis (an untested scientific explanation for a finding) about why this is the case. They believe that children in these environments have less exposure to bacterial infections during the first year of life than do poorer children. It is possible—but not proven—that living in a superclean environment results in a slightly weaker immune system.

Overall, cancer is rare in children. However, leukemia is the most common of all childhood cancers. Children and adolescents usually develop acute leukemia rather than chronic leukemia. About three out of four children and adolescents who develop leukemia have ALL. It is found most often in early childhood. ALL peaks between two and four years of age. While 90 percent of children with ALL are cured, adult survival is lower, ranging from 40 to 65 percent.

www.usatoday.com

USA TODAY

Life

SECTION D

February 24, 2010

From the Pages of USA TODAY

A bone marrow price tag?

Lawsuit argues that lives would be saved if donors were compensated

Should people be paid to donate bone marrow? About 20,000 bone marrow transplants are performed annually in the USA to treat disorders such as leukemia, and in 30% of cases, the donor is a relative, usually a sibling. The remaining transplants use marrow from volunteer donors, who are strangers to the recipients.

Although millions have registered to donate bone marrow, a lawsuit filed in California argues that too many patients are dying for want of a match. To encourage more prospective donors to sign up, the plaintiffs propose compensating bone marrow donors, a violation of the National Organ Transplant Act, which bans buying

ALL is a cancer of the lymphoblasts, the cells that come from the lymphoid stem cell. Normally, lymphoblasts turn into B cells (which make antibodies to fight infection). They also make T cells (which help B cells to make antibodies) and natural killer cells (which directly attack viruses and cancer cells). All of these cells are important parts of the body's immune system. There are several subtypes of ALL named for the cells that they affect. The most common subtype of ALL involves the lymphoblasts destined to turn into B cells. T-cell ALL is less common.

ALL starts when the DNA inside a single cell is damaged during normal cellular division. ALL can also develop when genes on chromosomes end up in the wrong place. Less often, the DNA in a donor organs, including bone marrow. The lawsuit argues that the government should not put bone marrow in the same category as solid organs such as kidneys. Bone marrow grows back, but kidneys do not, says the Washington, D.C. based Institute for Justice, which filed the suit.

Critics say financial incentives could lead people to cover up health problems that would make them ineligible to donate bone marrow. They worry that paying donors will discourage altruistic people from signing up, possibly leading to an overall decline in prospective donors.

Although it's illegal to compensate donors of blood meant for transfusion, Americans are allowed to sell plasma, the fluid part of blood used in making immunoglobulins and other treatments. People who sell plasma earn $20 to $30.

But research has shown that paid plasma donors have higher rates of infectious diseases than unpaid blood donors, John Miller, director of donor services for the National Marrow Donor Program says, suggesting that a similar problem might be seen with paid bone marrow donors. "We really want the safest product for the patient. When you pay people, they potentially have an incentive to not be as straightforward."

Because bone marrow produces immune system cells, finding a match is far trickier than with solid donor organs, says Jeffrey Chell, CEO of the National Marrow Donor Program. "The kind of matching we have to do is hundreds of millions of times more complex. There are literally more variations possible in the diversity we're looking for than there are people on Earth."

—*Rita Rubin*

cell is damaged by an outside source such as radiation. With ALL, abnormal lymphoblasts divide at an uncontrolled rate and fail to mature into normal lymphocytes. This causes the low number of healthy white blood cells associated with leukemia. It also causes the low counts of red blood cells and platelets, as those are crowded out by the lymphoblasts.

The symptoms of ALL—and other types of leukemia—are caused largely by the lack of normal white blood cells and too few red blood cells and platelets. Common symptoms include fever, infection, fatigue, anemia, bruising, and easy bleeding. With ALL, huge numbers of lymphoblasts accumulate inside the liver, the spleen, and especially the lymph nodes. Enlarged lymph nodes are common in

USA TODAY

ALL. Leukemia cells enter the brain and the spinal cord of about one in ten children with ALL. This can cause severe headaches, seizures, and problems with vision and balance. The abnormal cells also may collect in the testes of male patients. They can accumulate inside joints and on the surface of bones, causing severe pain.

The T-cell subtype of ALL may cause the thymus gland to enlarge. The thymus gland is part of the immune system. It's located in the middle of the chest behind the sternum. The thymus gland is fairly large in children and begins to shrink during the teen years. Adults have only a very small amount of thymus tissue remaining. However, when enlarged by T-cell ALL, the thymus presses on the trachea (windpipe). This causes coughing and breathing problems.

The thymus may become so swollen that it blocks the flow of blood in the veins. A large vein called the superior vena cava (SVC) returns blood from the body to the heart. When the enlarged thymus presses against the SVC, blood backs up in the veins. It causes severe swelling of the face, the arms, the neck, and the chest. This is called the SVC syndrome. It can be life-threatening and must be treated immediately.

Several of the tests used to diagnose leukemia give doctors an idea of a patient's prognosis—how likely the patient is to recover. Some of the factors that predict the prognosis for children with ALL include the following:

- Age—children with ALL between the ages of one and nine have better cure rates than do younger or older children.
- White blood cell count—the normal WBC count is five to ten thousand white blood cells per cubic millimeter of blood. Children with a WBC count of fifty thousand are high-risk and need more intensive treatment.
- Chromosome number—children have a better cure rate if their leukemia cells have more than fifty chromosomes instead

of the normal forty-six. Those with fewer than forty-six chromosomes have a less favorable outlook.

- Chromosome translocations—having the Philadelphia chromosome abnormality suggests a less favorable prognosis than other chromosome translocations.
- Response to treatment—children whose leukemia responds very well within one to two weeks of beginning treatment have a better outlook.

Some of the factors that help predict the prognosis for adults with ALL include the following:

- Age—patients under fifty years old generally do better than older patients.
- WBC count—adults with a WBC count less than thirty thousand for B-cell ALL and less than one hundred thousand for T-cell ALL have a better prognosis.
- Chromosome translocations—patients with the Philadelphia chromosome (found in 25 percent to 30 percent of adults with ALL) are likely to have a poorer prognosis.
- Response to treatment—adults who respond very well within four to five weeks of treatment have a better prognosis than people with a slower response.

ACUTE MYELOID LEUKEMIA

Acute myeloid leukemia is the second most common form of leukemia and the most dangerous. The lifetime risk of developing AML is 1 in 250 for men and 1 in 300 for women. About 1 out of 4 children and adolescents who have leukemia have AML. However, AML is much more common than ALL among adults. About 8 out of 10 adults with acute leukemia have AML. The incidence of AML

increases steadily with age, peaking among those over eighty years old. For unknown reasons, AML is more common in industrialized countries than in less developed countries.

Like other forms of leukemia, there is no specific cause for AML. It has been linked more strongly with exposure to the chemical benzene than ALL has. Because of improvements in industrial environments, there is less exposure to benzene in the workplace than years ago. Currently, cigarette smoke is the most common source of benzene exposure. AML also may be linked to chemotherapy or radiation given for another kind of cancer. When this happens, AML can develop one to five years after receiving chemotherapy. Still, most cases of AML cannot be directly traced to a specific cause.

AML results from a change in the DNA of a developing myeloid stem cell. The damaged stem cell quickly multiplies into eleven billion or more abnormal cells. These abnormal cells are called leukemic blasts. The blasts do not function normally, yet they reproduce and survive much better than healthy cells do. In fact, this is true of all forms of leukemia. The problem is not just the production of vast numbers of abnormal cells. The problem is also that the abnormal cells do not naturally die as normal cells do.

Healthy myeloid stem cells are destined to become red blood cells, platelets, and several kinds of white blood cells. People newly diagnosed with AML have a low number of healthy red blood cells, platelets, and white blood cells. Instead, they have vast numbers of leukemic white cells.

The symptoms of AML are similar to those of other forms of leukemia. People with AML are likely to have swollen gums, enlarged spleens or livers, and small infections and sores. People with AML can have episodes of severe bleeding because their platelet count is so low. They may have tiny red dots on the skin called petechiae, another sign of low platelets.

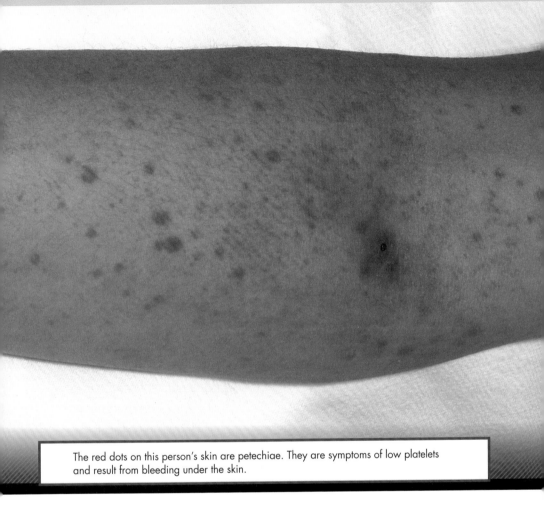

The red dots on this person's skin are petechiae. They are symptoms of low platelets and result from bleeding under the skin.

AML patients occasionally bleed into the brain or the lungs. This can be fatal if not treated quickly. A collection of AML cells can form outside of the bone marrow almost anywhere in the body. Younger patients seem to have a quicker onset of symptoms than do older people. Some children become dangerously ill in just one or two weeks. In an older person, a heart attack may be the first sign of AML. This happens because there are not enough red blood cells to carry sufficient oxygen to the heart.

AML, like ALL, has subtypes based on which cells are affected and what genetic abnormalities are found. Myeloid stem cells turn into a greater variety of cells than do lymphoid stem cells. AML is a cancer of one of these types of immature bone marrow cells:

- The cells that mature into red blood cells
- The cells that turn into megakaryocytes and then platelets
- The white blood cells that become monocytes and macrophages
- The white blood cells that form neutrophils, eosinophils, and basophils

Tests used to diagnose AML give doctors an idea of a patient's prognosis. These factors also guide the doctor in developing a treatment plan. For example, high-risk patients (depending on gender, white blood cell count, genetic abnormalities, and other factors described below) will receive more intensive treatment from the beginning than will those with average- or low-risk disease. Prognostic factors for children with AML include the following:

- White blood cell count—children with a white blood count higher than one hundred thousand have worse outcomes.
- Chromosome abnormalities—certain abnormal chromosomes predict a better outcome, while others suggest a less favorable outcome.
- Onset after cancer treatment—children who develop AML after treatment for another form of cancer generally have a worse outcome.
- Response to chemotherapy—children who respond quickly to one cycle of chemotherapy are more likely to be cured than those who take longer to respond or who do not respond at all.

The prognostic factors for adults with AML include these:

- Chromosome abnormalities—the primary predictor is which of the genetic and chromosomal abnormalities are present in any given patient.

- Age—the age at diagnosis is more important in adults than in children. Patients who are over sixty years old do not do as well as younger patients. Older patients may have more genetic abnormalities because of their age. Also, some older patients cannot tolerate the intensive chemotherapy treatments that may be required to treat AML.
- White blood cell count—having a white blood count above one hundred thousand suggests a less favorable outcome.

Estimated New Cases of Leukemia in 2010

	Number of Cases	Number of Deaths
All forms of leukemia	43,050	21,840
Acute lymphocytic leukemia	5,330	1,420
Acute myeloid leukemia	12,330	8,950
Chronic lymphocytic leukemia	14,990	4,390
Chronic myeloid leukemia	4,870	440
All other forms of leukemia	5,530	6,640*

Source: American Cancer Society

*The higher number of deaths than cases may reflect undercounting case estimates or inexact reporting on death certificates.

CHRONIC LYMPHOCYTIC LEUKEMIA

Chronic lymphocytic leukemia is the most common form of leukemia. Overall, it accounts for about one-third of all cases of leukemia. A person's lifetime risk of developing CLL is one in two hundred. CLL is extremely rare in children, so nearly every case occurs in adults. Like other forms of leukemia, CLL becomes more common with age. Most cases of CLL occur among people who are over fifty-five years old. The average age at diagnosis is about seventy-two years old.

CLL involves the lymphoid stem cells and lymphoblasts. It starts with a genetic mutation in one single cell while it is still within the bone marrow. Most cases of CLL affect the B lymphocyte. Less often CLL affects the T lymphocyte. Instead of becoming a normal B or T lymphocyte, the abnormal cell clones itself over and over. The genetically damaged cells are hardier than normal cells, and over time, they crowd out the normal cells.

Even though CLL is a chronic leukemia, patients may have a form of CLL that develops rapidly or slowly. Lymphocytes are an important part of the immune system. The lack of healthy T and B lymphocytes means that people with the faster-growing form of CLL are very likely to suffer from frequent infections. These range from minor cold sores caused by herpes viruses to more serious bacterial infections of the lungs and the kidneys. Most patients who go to their doctors with symptoms have swollen lymph nodes when they are diagnosed with CLL. These nodes may press on other organs such as the bladder or the stomach. Patients may also have fever, chills, night sweats, and weight loss. Many people will have enlarged spleens and livers as well.

Other people have the slower-growing form of CLL and may experience few if any symptoms for years. In fact, up to half of all patients with CLL have no symptoms when the disease is discovered.

They may have gone to the doctor for a routine physical exam, including blood work such as a complete blood count and tests for cholesterol and diabetes. Laboratory technicians discover abnormal lymphocytes or too many lymphocytes when they look at the white blood cells under a microscope.

As with other types of leukemia, doctors cannot be sure why one person develops CLL and another does not. However, two risk factors seem to be important. One is exposure to Agent Orange, the mix of

Agent Orange and Vietnam War Veterans

Vietnam veterans may be eligible for disability payments and health-care benefits for diseases that the Veterans Administration recognizes as being associated with exposure to Agent Orange. Spouses and children of veterans who died as the result of diseases associated with Agent Orange may be eligible for survivor's benefits. A partial listing of recognized diseases includes:

Chronic lymphocytic leukemia

Diabetes mellitus (type 2)

Hodgkin's disease

Ischemic heart disease

Multiple myeloma

Non-Hodgkin's lymphoma

Parkinson's disease

Peripheral neuropathy

Prostate cancer

Respiratory cancers (lung, larynx, and trachea)

Source: www.publichealth.va.gov/exposures/agentorange/diseases.asp

herbicides used in the Vietnam War that has been recognized as a cause of CLL. Other herbicides or pesticides may also contribute to CLL, but they have not been proven to do so.

The other risk factor for developing CLL is family history. First-degree relatives (parents, children, and siblings) of CLL patients are two to four times more likely to develop it than are people who do not have relatives with CLL. This is the only significant family connection—other than in identical twins—that any form of leukemia has.

CHRONIC MYELOID LEUKEMIA

Chronic myeloid leukemia is almost exclusively found in adults. Fewer than fifty cases are diagnosed in American children each year. (Jake Owen, introduced in the previous chapter, is one of those children). Overall, CML is a rare form of leukemia. A person's lifetime risk of developing CML is 1 in 625. As with other forms of leukemia, more men than women get it. It is more common among whites than African Americans. CML occurs more often among the middle-aged than the young or very elderly. The average age at diagnosis is sixty-six years old.

The genetic cause of CML is better understood than that of any other kind of leukemia. About 95 percent of the people who develop CML have one specific chromosomal abnormality, the Philadephia chromosome. Scientists number each of the twenty-three pairs of chromosomes in a human cell so they can identify abnormalities such as this one. They found that during cellular division in CML patients, a piece of chromosome 9 moves to chromosome 22 and vice versa. The result is a shorter-than-normal chromosome 22 called the Philadelphia chromosome. Scientists think this error happens because the chromosomes are close to each other.

The swapping of chromosome segments to create the Philadelphia chromosome leads to the formation of a new gene—a cancer-promoting oncogene. This gene produces an abnormal protein called tyrosine kinase. The protein allows CML cells to grow and reproduce without control. The identification of tyrosine kinase allowed researchers to develop a class of medication that inhibits or slows the abnormal protein. This keeps the CML cells from uncontrolled reproduction and makes CML the easiest form of leukemia to treat.

The symptoms of CML are very similar to those for other forms of leukemia. As with CLL, many patients will have no symptoms at first. Of those who do, an enlarged spleen is the most common. An enlarged liver is less common. Other symptoms include fatigue, anemia, shortness of breath, night sweats, and weight loss.

Signs of a poor outcome for patients with CML include these:
- Having an enlarged spleen
- Having areas of bone damaged by leukemia cells
- Having very high or very low platelet counts
- Being sixty years old or more
- Being in the accelerated or blast phase (described below)

CML has three clearly defined stages. They are known as chronic, accelerated, and blast phase.

In the chronic phase, the patient may not know that he has leukemia at this phase. His symptoms are mild, and he has fewer than 10 percent myeloid blasts in his blood or bone marrow. Myeloid blasts create red blood cells, platelets, and some white blood cells. Patients often respond well to treatment in this phase.

During the accelerated phase, the patient has between 10 percent and 20 percent myeloid blasts in her blood or bone marrow. She also has a greatly increased or decreased number of white blood cells, very high or low platelets, and mutations in chromosomes.

Once the patient has reached blast phase, he has more than 20 percent myeloid blasts, which have spread to his tissues and organs. He may have fever, breathing problems, infection, or bleeding. At this point, CML acts more like an acute form of leukemia than a chronic form. People in this phase are unlikely to respond to treatment. They may live six months or less.

OTHER FORMS OF LEUKEMIA

There are a few other types of leukemia that are rare or that are subtypes of ALL, AML, CLL, or CML. For example, hairy cell leukemia is a slow-growing form of chronic lymphocytic leukemia that affects about eight hundred people in the United States each year. It is called hairy cell leukemia because the leukemic lymphocytes have tiny projections that look like hairs when viewed under a microscope.

Another rare leukemia is acute promyelocytic leukemia (APL), the type that Yvonne Schmidt has. APL is a subtype of AML. It strikes about six hundred Americans each year. The median age for APL is forty years, while AML is most often found in much older people. People with APL may experience serious, life-threatening bleeding due to an extremely short supply of healthy red blood cells and platelets. APL is sometimes classified by itself because it acts differently than AML and requires different treatment.

Some other types of leukemia are poorly identified or lie in a gray zone between leukemia and lymphoma (cancer of the lymph nodes). All together, over forty-three thousand people are diagnosed with leukemia each year in the United States. While the number of people developing leukemia has remained about the same for many years, new and better treatments are steadily improving survival rates.

FINALLY, NEWLYWED LIFE

After three rounds of chemotherapy, doctors told Yvonne that her leukemia was in remission. After six months, she felt well enough to return to work. She also took college classes to become an occupational therapist. Yvonne was an active woman. She ran marathons and had a brown belt in martial arts. She walked every day to get her strength back. With medication helping to keep her leukemia at bay, things were looking pretty good. "We're finally starting to live a normal newlywed life," she said. "It's a good feeling."

USA TODAY

CHAPTER SIX

TREATING LEUKEMIA

When two-year-old Montana Oatman seemed too tired to play, his parents got worried. He was not the active, playful toddler they knew. "We could tell something was wrong because he wanted to go to bed at five o'clock at night," Montana's dad said. Two doctors thought Montana had the flu because he was weak and sleeping so much. The third doctor ordered a blood test. It showed that Montana had the form of leukemia called acute lymphocytic leukemia, the most common type of leukemia in children.

"When we found out, it was so shocking," Montana's mom said. The doctor told Montana's parents to take him to St. Jude Children's Research Hospital in Memphis, Tennessee. St. Jude's is one of the most well-known children's hospitals in the nation. At the hospital, specialists in childhood leukemia designed a treatment plan for Montana. After just three weeks of chemotherapy, he was in remission. But Montana would need to complete three years of treatment for the best chance of a full recovery.

Before beginning treatment for leukemia, doctors must identify exactly what form of leukemia a person has. They must discover which specific chromosomal and genetic abnormalities are present. Other factors doctors must consider before developing a treatment plan are these:

- How old is the patient? Children and adults may need different medications and varying lengths of treatment. Younger people generally can tolerate intensive treatment better than older people.
- What is the gender? Young boys with ALL are typically treated longer than young girls with ALL. Adult males with CLL generally don't do as well as adult females.

- Have cancerous white blood cells spread into the lymph nodes, the spleen, the liver, the spine, or the brain?
- How much of the bone marrow is affected?
- Is this the first treatment for the patient, or has the patient been treated before and is now experiencing a relapse?
- Do blood tests show an unusually high number of cancerous white blood cells?
- Are there a very low number of red blood cells and platelets?
- Does the patient have other illnesses or conditions that may affect treatment?

When possible, people who have leukemia should be treated in specialized cancer centers where the staff is familiar with the complexities of the disease. There are dozens of such centers across the United States. Many are associated with major universities or large hospitals. Some specialize in treating only children. Cancer centers are usually in big cities. They may provide housing for parents, siblings, and spouses of patients.

Treatment for some forms of leukemia is very difficult and takes many months. Some treatments, such as chemotherapy, are used for all types of leukemia. Other treatments and medications are specialized and are used for just one kind of leukemia.

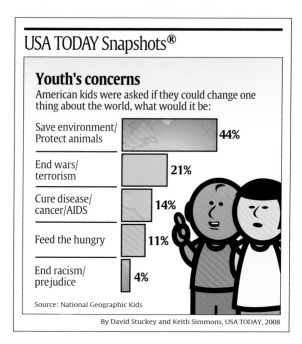

USA TODAY Snapshots®

Youth's concerns
American kids were asked if they could change one thing about the world, what would it be:

Save environment/ Protect animals	44%
End wars/ terrorism	21%
Cure disease/ cancer/AIDS	14%
Feed the hungry	11%
End racism/ prejudice	4%

Source: National Geographic Kids

By David Stuckey and Keith Simmons, USA TODAY, 2008

CHEMOTHERAPY

Chemotherapy is the most common way to treat leukemia. There are dozens of chemotherapy medications. Some of these powerful drugs directly attack and kill the leukemia cells. Other drugs stop the cells from dividing. Most chemotherapy is given through a needle inserted into a patient's vein. Some kinds of chemotherapy come in pills. It also may be necessary to inject chemotherapy medications into the spinal canal. This process is called intrathecal therapy. Doctors give chemotherapy in phases.

CHEMOTHERAPY FOR ACUTE LYMPHOCYTIC LEUKEMIA

Induction therapy is the first phase of chemotherapy for ALL. The doctor gives large doses of drugs to kill as many leukemia cells as possible as quickly as possible. Patients with ALL often receive a combination of two or more different drugs for four to six weeks

Phases of Chemotherapy

Chemotherapy for Acute Lymphocytic Leukemia

    1. Induction

    2. Consolidation

    3. Maintenance

Chemotherapy for Acute Myeloid Leukemia

    1. Induction

    2. Consolidation

during this phase. Giving several medications strengthens the effects of the chemotherapy. More leukemia cells are killed when several drugs are used together. Using several drugs also reduces the chance of the leukemia becoming resistant to any one drug.

The goal of induction chemotherapy is to achieve a remission. A complete remission means that all signs of leukemia have disappeared. A partial remission means that the leukemia is greatly improved, but leukemia cells can still be found. More than 95 percent of children with ALL enter partial remission and begin feeling better after just one month of treatment. However, it is possible that the leukemia might return after remission. Chemotherapy alone cures some, but not all, patients with ALL.

Consolidation therapy is the second phase of treatment for ALL. By the time a doctor discovers that a patient has leukemia, the patient's body may harbor one hundred billion leukemia cells. Induction therapy kills over 99 percent of those cells. This still leaves about one hundred million leukemia cells in the body. Those cells must be killed as well so that the leukemia does not return. The consolidation stage lasts four to eight weeks. Its purpose is to further reduce the number of leukemia cells remaining in a patient's body. Different drugs may be used during this phase or lower doses of the same drugs, depending on the protocols (procedures) used in a particular cancer center.

In many patients with ALL, the leukemic cells will have reached the brain or the spinal cord. These cells must be killed with intrathecal chemotherapy. The blood-brain barrier keeps most medications from reaching the brain and the spinal cord. Injecting medications directly into the cerebrospinal fluid is the only way to kill leukemia cells that have reached those areas. The doctor inserts a needle into the spinal canal and injects chemotherapy medications. Intrathecal chemotherapy begins during the induction phase and may last into the consolidation phase. It may be performed six to eight times during the first few months of treatment.

Maintenance therapy is the third phase of chemotherapy for ALL patients. Many patients are in remission at the end of the first two phases of treatment. Children with ALL will receive maintenance therapy for two to three years. Boys are at higher risk for relapse than girls, so they are usually treated longer than girls. During this phase, the patient may take medications by mouth and receive others intravenously every few weeks. This stage may include drugs not given during the induction and consolidation phases. The drugs used depend on treatment protocols, how patients respond, and the chromosomal and genetic characteristics of a patient's leukemia.

Children with ALL respond better to chemotherapy than adults do. Chemotherapy alone cures far more children with ALL than

Chemotherapy Drugs for Acute Leukemia

Drugs commonly used to treat ALL and AML include these:

- carboplatin
- cyclophosphamide
- cytarabine
- daunorubicin
- doxorubicin
- etoposide

- hydroxyurea
- L-asparaginase
- methotrexate
- 6-mercaptopurine
- teniposide
- vincristine

adults. People who are not cured or who relapse will need additional chemotherapy. They also may require a stem cell transplant for a cure.

CHEMOTHERAPY FOR ACUTE MYELOID LEUKEMIA

Treatment for AML involves two phases. The first phase of chemotherapy for AML is also called the induction phase. During the induction phase, two medications are given for several days in a row. The patient is allowed time to recover, and then the medications may be repeated again in two weeks. Patients who do not respond well may receive additional rounds of medication. Treatment is repeated until the bone marrow shows no more leukemia cells and is producing healthy blood cells (red blood cells, platelets, and normal white blood cells). This usually takes two to three treatments.

The second phase of treatment for AML is consolidation, which begins when the bone marrow shows no visible leukemia cells. The patient receives high doses of one or two chemotherapy drugs for several months. Like patients with ALL, patients with AML often require intrathecal chemotherapy. If patients stay in remission, no further treatment may be needed. However, stem cell transplants may be required if the patient relapses or does not respond well to chemotherapy.

CHEMOTHERAPY TREATMENT FOR CHRONIC LEUKEMIA

Chronic lymphocytic leukemia and chronic myeloid leukemia cannot be cured with chemotherapy alone. Patients with these two forms of chronic leukemia may not initially require any treatment at all. Instead, the doctor may take a watch-and-wait approach. The doctor performs blood tests every few months to see if the leukemia is progressing. Many patients with chronic leukemia have few if any symptoms for several years. They will not require immediate treatment.

December 14, 2005

From the Pages of USA TODAY

'Targeted' cancer treatment effective in older patients

Patients over 50 make up the bulk of those diagnosed with cancer. Yet these patients are often considered too old and frail for potentially lifesaving treatments such as bone-marrow transplants, says John Pagel, a blood cancer specialist at the Fred Hutchinson Cancer Research Center in Seattle.

"If we could get enough therapy into people, we could cure them," Pagel says. Pagel and others are experimenting with methods that "target" cancer cells more precisely. His team focused on patients 50 and older who had either acute myeloid leukemia or myelodysplastic syndrome, a condition that often leads to cancer.

Instead of exposing the body to radiation, which can injure vital organs, scientists attached radioactive particles to man-made versions of immune system proteins called antibodies. The antibodies were engineered to stick only to the types of white blood cells that are afflicted by these cancers. That brings radiation directly to tumor cells but mostly spares other parts of the body.

Because doctors targeted cancerous tissue, they were able to give much stronger doses. In the study, about 55% of the patients were alive after about 10 months. Without treatment, all of the patients were expected to die from their disease, Pagel says.

Thomas Shea, director of bone-marrow transplantation at the University of North Carolina Comprehensive Cancer Center in Chapel Hill, says, "Not only can older patients tolerate these treatments well, but they had a good response."

—Liz Szabo

Eventually, most patients with chronic leukemia will require treatment. The doctor may decide to begin treatment for CLL when there is a rapid increase in abnormal lymphocytes. He will also begin treatment if the patient has severe anemia or low platelets or if the lymph nodes and the spleen start to enlarge. Some of the chemotherapy medications used to treat ALL and AML are also used to treat CLL. Other medications used for CLL are fludarabine, bendamustine, chlorambucil, and cyclophosphamide. Doctors believe stem cell transplants are the only cure for CLL.

Chemotherapy is not often used to treat CML because tyrosine kinase inhibitors are available and work better. Chemotherapy may be needed if the tyrosine kinase inhibitors are no longer effective. When required, chemotherapy for CML includes hydroxyurea, cytarabine, busulfan, vincristine, and cyclophosphamide.

Chemotherapy works by killing fast-growing leukemia cells. This causes many side effects because other cells in the body also divide quickly. These include cells in the bone marrow; the lining of the mouth, stomach, and intestines; and the hair follicles. Medications can help control some of the side effects. Common side effects of chemotherapy include these:

- Hair loss (because hair follicles are damaged or killed)
- Mouth sores, loss of appetite, nausea, and vomiting (chemotherapy damages the rapidly growing cells that line the intestinal tract)
- Increased risk of infections (due to low numbers of healthy white blood cells)
- Easy bruising (due to low platelet count)
- Fatigue (due to low numbers of red blood cells)

People who have chemotherapy may have trouble conceiving a child in the future because the medications can damage ovaries and testes. The younger a patient is, especially if he or she has not yet reached puberty, the better the chance of retaining fertility as an adult. Some children who receive chemotherapy may experience a delay in growth. They may catch up over time and reach their full height over a period of several years after the treatment is over.

www.usatoday.com

Life

SECTION D

May 4, 2005

From the Pages of USA TODAY

Survival isn't child's play

For young patients who are cured, the fallout can be frustrating

Although childhood cancer is now largely curable, experts say efforts to prevent and treat side-effects of treatment—which can include lifelong learning disabilities—have progressed slowly.

Like many young patients, Moe Freeman says he finished cancer treatment in the 8th grade and found it had eroded his short-term memory and concentration. He still excelled in drama and charmed his way through productions, improvising when he forgot his lines. But he was frustrated by the loss of his ability to translate his thoughts into writing. "I knew all the answers," he says, "but come test time, I'd bomb out."

Kids often have a tough time after treatment, says Debra Abney of the Leukemia and Lymphoma Society. "Pediatric cancer is relatively rare, so many educators are unfamiliar with their needs. The kids look healthy, so when they start having problems, people think they're just disorganized."

Freeman's problems followed him to his first job at a Dairy Queen when he was in high school. "My manager would ask me to mop the floor, and I'd have to ask how. I'd hook up the bucket wrong, and water would spill all over the floor."

Doctors are working on ways to scale back therapy, hoping less intensive treatments will spare children from complications. Most leukemia patients, for example, are now treated with chemotherapy alone and skip radiation, says Daniel Armstrong, director of the Mailman Center for Child Development at the University of Miami.

Researchers also are learning how to help cancer survivors compensate for their disabilities. Alma Morgan, educational consultant at the Medical College of Virginia, recommends that parents work with schools to develop programs to include special education classes or accommodations tailored to cancer survivors' needs. Experts say that cancer survivors and their families need emotional and social support to make it through school.

—Liz Szabo

Children who have radiation in addition to chemotherapy are less likely to reach their full adult height.

Tumor lysis syndrome is another potential side effect of chemotherapy. *Lysis* means "the breakdown of cells." Chemotherapy kills vast numbers of white blood cells within the first hours and days of treatment. When the cells die, they release their contents into the bloodstream. The kidneys cleanse waste products from the blood. But when tumor lysis syndrome occurs, they cannot excrete all the cellular waste products quickly enough. There is too much potassium, phosphate, uric acid, and other chemicals in the blood. The build-up of these minerals and chemicals may lead to sudden kidney failure. Chemical imbalances can also cause dangerous irregular heartbeats. Tumor lysis syndrome is most common with patients with ALL and AML. It is very serious. Doctors treat tumor lysis syndrome with large amounts of intravenous fluids. They also give medications that counteract the effects of the cellular waste products.

OTHER MEDICATIONS

TYROSINE KINASE INHIBITORS

Tyrosine kinase inhibitors are more effective at treating CML than chemotherapy is, because they control the abnormal protein associated with the Philadelphia chromosome (most often found in CML patients). The chromosome causes a new cancer-promoting oncogene to form. This oncogene produces a protein called tyrosine kinase that allows leukemia cells to grow unchecked. Tyrosine kinase inhibitors stop or slow down the growth of leukemia cells by attacking the protein.

Imatinib (brand name Gleevec) was the first of these tyrosine kinase inhibitors. Gleevec has been spectacularly successful at helping people with CML within weeks. Gleevec may work for ten years or more for some patients before their leukemia becomes resistant to it. Two newer drugs that work in the same way are dasatinib (Sprycel) and nilotinib (Tasigna). These drugs may help people if they cannot take Gleevec or if their leukemia has become resistant to it. Some patients show an even better response to the new drugs. Studies released in 2010 suggest they will become standard therapy for CML.

Tyrosine kinase inhibitors have far fewer side effects than does chemotherapy. Chemotherapy damages healthy cells as well as cancerous cells. However, targeted therapy, such as the tyrosine kinase inhibitors, affects only the cancerous cells. These drugs, which are given by mouth, may cause muscle pain, fatigue, nausea, diarrhea, and skin rashes. Occasionally, patients may have swelling of their arms, legs, and faces caused by excess fluid in body tissues. Even so, tyrosine kinase inhibitors provide a safe and successful treatment for a once-deadly condition.

A study published in the medical journal *Lancet Oncology* found that tyrosine kinase inhibitors might fully cure some patients with CML. The study followed one hundred patients who had been on Gleevec for CML. Their bodies showed no sign of leukemia while on the medication. Doctors stopped the medication and checked on the patients monthly for two or more years. One year after stopping Gleevec, 41 percent of patients showed no sign of leukemia. Two years after stopping Gleevec, 38 percent remained free of leukemia. Doctors say that while the study involved a small number of people, it appears that tyrosine kinase inhibitors might cure CML in some patients.

INTERFERON

The immune system naturally makes substances called interferons that help the body fight infections and cancer. However, when someone has leukemia, the body needs more interferon than it can make. Scientists developed synthetic versions of interferon that reduce the growth of leukemia cells. Interferon was once the main treatment for CML, but tyrosine kinase inhibitors are currently the first-line treatment. If those medications no longer help or if a patient cannot take them, she may receive interferon for several years to control her CML. Interferon is injected under the skin once a day. It has serious side effects that include severe flulike symptoms (muscle aches, bone pain, fever, and fatigue). Interferon can also lead to mental and emotional problems such as depression, confusion, anxiety, and poor concentration.

MONOCLONAL ANTIBODIES

Monoclonal antibodies are synthetic versions of antibodies, the proteins made by our immune system that attack foreign proteins (antigens). Scientists have designed monoclonal antibodies that attach to an abnormal antigen on the surface of leukemia cells. They are used to treat CLL by themselves or in combination with chemotherapy. The most commonly used monoclonal antibody for CLL is called rituximab (Rituxan). It is injected into a vein once a week. Other than the risk of an allergic reaction, side effects are few. It may cause tumor lysis syndrome in patients with very high numbers of white blood cells. Studies show that using Rituxan along with standard chemotherapy significantly increases survival.

Steroids. Steroids are a class of drugs given along with chemotherapy to help kill the leukemia cells. These are usually given in tablets a few days each month. Steroids include prednisolone, prednisone, and dexamethasone. Steroids may cause the body to retain extra fluid. They are the primary reason some people with leukemia have puffy faces and gain weight. Steroids are powerful medications, but they carry the risk of serious side effects. These include an increased chance of infections, weakening of the bones, and mood changes (such as depression and irritability).

Antibiotics and antifungals. A healthy immune system successfully overcomes many bacterial and fungal infections. But patients with leukemia easily develop infections because they have weakened immune systems. Receiving chemotherapy also weakens the immune system. This adds up to a dangerous double whammy. All leukemia patients who develop fevers receive antibiotics—medications that fight bacterial infections. Some patients undergoing intensive chemotherapy receive antibiotics as a preventive measure even if they do not have a fever. Patients who do not improve after several days of antibiotics often receive antifungal medications. Fungi such as *aspergillus* can cause lung infections in patients with poor immune systems.

RADIATION THERAPY

Radiation therapy is not used as often in leukemia patients as with other kinds of cancer. The most common use of radiation in the treatment of leukemia is just before a stem cell transplant. However, radiation is also used to help shrink enlarged spleens or a thymus gland that is putting pressure on nearby organs. Radiation can be used to treat bone pain by killing some of the leukemia cells within the bone if chemotherapy does not help. It may be used to treat leukemia if it has spread to the brain and the spinal fluid.

Radiation is generally given five times a week for six to eight weeks. Side effects depend on what part of the body receives the radiation. For example, radiation to the abdomen can cause nausea, vomiting, and diarrhea. Skin at the site may become dry, red, and irritated. Temporary or permanent infertility may occur if the radiation affects the ovaries or the testes.

BLOOD PRODUCTS AND BLOOD TREATMENTS

Patients with acute leukemia (ALL or AML) cannot produce enough red blood cells or platelets. Chemotherapy can make the shortage of these vital cells even worse. Patients with very low numbers of red blood cells receive blood transfusions. This helps to prevent heart and lung problems that develop when the body does not get enough oxygen. Patients with very low numbers of platelets receive transfusions of platelets to prevent hemorrhages into the lungs, the brain, or the gastrointestinal tract. If a patient has low levels of certain proteins that help blood to clot, a doctor may give him a blood product called fresh frozen plasma to prevent bleeding.

Before blood products are given to patients with leukemia, they must be irradiated—treated with radiation. This prevents graft-versus-host disease. In this disease, the immune cells of a graft (in this case, the blood transfusion) attack the host (the leukemia patient). Graft-versus-host disease can be fatal to leukemia patients.

Many leukemia patients have vast numbers of abnormal white blood cells circulating through their bodies. In some cases, doctors must remove some of the cells before starting leukemia treatment. The abnormal white blood cells slow blood flow to the brain, the lungs, the eyes, and other organs. The abnormal cells become a kind of sludge that blocks and damages tiny blood vessels. Patients are hooked up to a machine similar to the dialysis machine used to clean blood for patients with kidney failure. The process, called leukapheresis, removes excessive white blood cells from the blood. The cleansed blood is returned to the patient. Leukapheresis treatment takes three to four hours and only temporarily relieves symptoms.

Because chemotherapy kills white blood cells that fight infection, receiving chemotherapy puts patients at great risk for infections. Patients can receive medications called growth stimulating factors during chemotherapy. These medications stimulate the production of healthy white blood cells. Patients who receive growth stimulating factors have fewer infections. They often recover from chemotherapy faster than patients who do not receive the medications.

SURGERY

While surgery is widely used in many cancer treatments, it is used much less often with leukemia. Patients with cancers that form solid tumors (for example, lung cancer) require surgery to remove the tumor. Leukemia is a cancer of the blood and bone marrow. Solid tumors are not part of the disease process. Most patients with leukemia need a minor surgical procedure to insert intravenous lines into big veins in the neck or the chest. These lines allow the medical staff to draw blood and to give medications without having to stick the patient with needles.

Some leukemia patients need surgery to remove their spleens. The spleen normally traps damaged red blood cells and platelets. In patients with leukemia, the spleen enlarges because it traps many more damaged and abnormal blood cells than usual. As the spleen gets bigger, it begins to trap normal cells along with the abnormal cells, becoming even larger and capable of trapping even more cells. Ultimately, the spleen removes too many red blood cells and platelets from the circulation. This leaves patients with severe anemia and puts them at risk of serious bleeding. Sometimes a spleen becomes so large it puts painful pressure on nearby organs. If chemotherapy or radiation does not shrink the spleen, surgeons will likely remove it. Most people have no problems living without a spleen. The primary complication is an increased risk of infections.

Chemotherapy alone cures between 75 percent and 80 percent of children with ALL. It cures only about 30 percent to 40 percent of adults with ALL. Chemotherapy cures a minority of patients with AML. It cannot cure CLL or CML at all. When chemotherapy and other medications fail to cure leukemia, some patients go on to receive stem cell transplants. As you'll read in the next chapter, these potentially lifesaving transplants are risky and complex but offer the only chance for a cure for many people.

STRENGTH IN RECOVERY

Montana received most of his chemotherapy at home but returned to St. Jude's every two months for checkups and tests. He lost his hair due to chemotherapy. Steroids caused his body to swell and gave him mood swings. The chemotherapy was so hard on Montana's joints that he had to learn how to walk all over again. "His strength is incredible," said his mother, Jessica Oatman, a professional photographer. She is one of a group of photographers who photograph children with cancer for their families. "I want to document what these children go through. Years later, no matter what happens, these images will be the memory of a hero." She shares some of the photos with the public at the website Images of Hope (www.hopeconquers.org).

CHAPTER SEVEN

STEM CELL TRANSPLANTS

Michael Billig, forty-three years old and in good shape, clocked several hours of running each week. He noticed that it was harder and harder to finish his run. Sometimes he had to walk home. Michael thought he was overtraining. But even slowing his pace didn't help very much. Then he started to become short of breath. That was enough to send him to his doctor. Michael first thought he had the flu or maybe Lyme disease. Instead, the doctor told Michael that he had chronic lymphocytic leukemia, the most common form of leukemia.

When Michael got the news, he collapsed in a chair in stunned silence. "I thought of my daughters, my wife of four months, all the things I had yet to do in life," he said. CLL had taken over 90 percent of Michael's blood. His doctors said Michael had a very aggressive form of CLL that needed immediate treatment. He started several rounds of chemotherapy at the renowned Johns Hopkins Hospital in Baltimore, Maryland. He would later need a new type of stem cell transplant.

Chemotherapy alone cures a majority of young children who have acute lymphocytic leukemia. It also cures a small number of people with acute myeloid leukemia. But chemotherapy cannot cure the rest of the people with ALL and AML. And chemotherapy cannot cure chronic forms of leukemia. When chemotherapy and other treatments fail to cure or control a person's leukemia, a stem cell transplant may offer the only chance of survival.

Stem cells are unspecialized cells with the ability to develop into other types of cells. They differ from other cells because they can divide and renew themselves indefinitely. Inside the bone marrow, blood stem cells produce myeloid and lymphoid stem cells. In healthy people, these cells go on to become all the different types of blood cells that keep us alive. If a genetic mutation occurs in just one myeloid or lymphoid stem cell, that cell produces billions of mutated cells exactly like itself. That happens when someone has leukemia.

STEM CELL SOURCES

Stem cell transplants are either autologous—coming from the patient's own body—or allogeneic—coming from another person. There are advantages and disadvantages to each type of transplant. An allogeneic stem cell transplant requires a closely matched donor. Proteins called human leukocyte antigens (HLA) live on the surface of most cells. There are several major groups of HLA that give each person a unique tissue type.

An exact HLA match occurs only in identical twins or other identical multiple births. Siblings who have the same biological parents (not half-siblings) have a 25 percent chance of being an excellent match. People who do not have identical twins or an HLA-matched sibling must receive a transplant from the most closely matched donor possible. Allogeneic stem cell transplants have two disadvantages. The first disadvantage is the difficulty with finding a well-matched donor. The second is the chance of graft-versus-host disease, in which donor cells attack the patient.

In an autologous stem cell transplant, doctors remove stem cells from the patient's own bone marrow or bloodstream. They give the patient intensive chemotherapy to try to kill all remaining leukemia cells in the body. They may also use radiation for this purpose as well. The stem cells that the doctors remove from the patient may be treated in an attempt to kill all leukemia cells. When a patient's own stem cells are used, there is no chance of graft-versus-host disease. The body recognizes its own cells and does not attack them. An autologous stem cell transplant has one great disadvantage. Despite attempts to clear the transplant of leukemia cells, some might remain in the patient's body and in the stem cells returned to the patient. This means the transplant would not cure the patient. Instead, the leukemia would return.

It used to be that when doctors talked about a stem cell transplant for leukemia, they meant a bone marrow transplant. Bone marrow is still the most common source of stem cells. But science is increasingly mining a variety of stem cell sources to provide a broader range of treatment choices.

The colored micrograph shows a bone marrow stem cell from adult bone marrow. A bone marrow stem cell makes several types of cells including white blood cells and red blood cells.

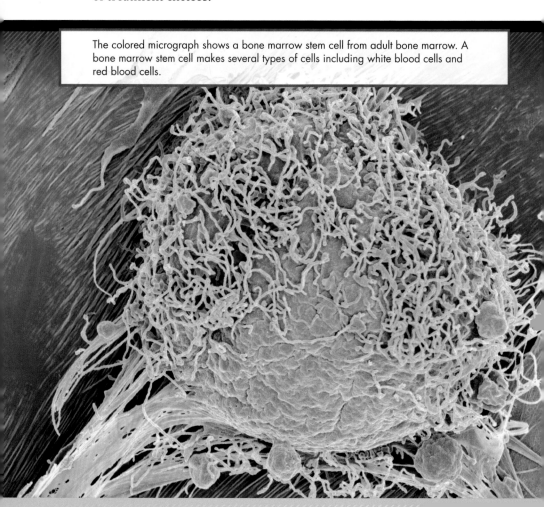

BONE MARROW

Bone marrow is where stem cells and new blood cells form. An infusion of healthy stem cells is the only way to cure many leukemia patients. Dr. E. Donnall Thomas at the Fred Hutchinson Cancer Research Center in Seattle, Washington, pioneered bone marrow transplants from the 1950s through the 1970s. Thomas showed that the stem cells in healthy bone marrow could repopulate the cancerous bone marrow of patients with leukemia. He won a Nobel Prize for his work.

Doctors look for a perfect or near-perfect HLA match when they plan a bone marrow transplant. The donor receives anesthesia prior to "harvesting" the bone marrow. During the harvesting, the doctor inserts a large needle into the back of the hip bone. She then withdraws about 1 to 6 cups (350 to 1,500 milliliters) of the donor's marrow. A smaller amount of marrow would be drawn from a child donor, for example, in a twin or sibling donation. The procedure takes one to two hours.

The marrow is processed to remove bone fragments, fat, and other debris. It may be given immediately to the patient or frozen until the patient is ready for the transplant. The donor may remain in the hospital for

Doctors remove bone marrow from a donor for a transplant. The donor needs to be a close HLA match to the recipient for the best chance of success.

Becoming a Donor

Did you ever think that you could save a life? Anyone between the ages of eighteen and sixty can register to become a bone marrow donor. The sign-up process starts with a simple cheek swab and a health questionnaire. Donors must be free of cancer, heart disease, hepatitis, HIV, and a number of other conditions.

If your cells are a match for a patient in need, you will be asked to have further tests. This may require blood tests and a physical examination. In about three out of four cases, bone marrow itself is not actually required. Instead, doctors collect peripheral stem cells to give to the patient.

The donor must get injections for several days to stimulate production of bone marrow stem cells. The injections may cause headaches, bone pain, and flu-like symptoms that soon resolve. Then it may take a total of eight hours or so for the stem cells to be collected from the donor. There are no costs to the donor. The patient's insurance pays transportation and medical costs.

The donor and the patient are not allowed to know each other's names for the first year. After that time, if both parties agree, the National Marrow Donor Program can put the donor and patient in touch with each other. Imagine meeting the person who received your lifesaving stem cells! What would that feel like?

several hours or overnight. The donor will be bruised and sore for a few days after the harvest. Usually, over-the-counter medications such as ibuprofen are enough to control the pain. The donor's body replaces its missing bone marrow within four to six weeks.

UMBILICAL CORD BLOOD

The umbilical cord connects a newborn infant to its mother. It runs from the fetus's umbilicus (belly button) to the mother's placenta inside the uterus. The cord is cut shortly after delivery to separate the placenta and baby. In the past, the cord and the placenta were dumped as medical waste. Doctors now know that cord blood is rich in stem cells.

While many cords are still discarded, some hospitals now ask new mothers to donate their baby's cord blood for use in stem cell transplants. Some parents choose to save the cord blood in a family cord blood bank in case their own child should need it in the future. Many doctors encourage parents to instead donate cord blood to a public bank which serves all patients. The chance of any one child later needing its own cord blood is very small. The chance of another child needing it is much greater.

In a cord blood donation, a hospital technician or doctor takes about 75 milliliters (0.3 cups) of blood from one infant's cord and placenta. That is called one cord blood unit. One unit may provide enough stem cells for a transplant. However, an adult often requires at least two cord blood units.

One advantage of cord blood transplant is that the donor and the recipient do not have to be as closely matched as do bone marrow donors and recipients. Stem cells in cord blood more readily adapt to a new environment—the patient—than do bone marrow stem cells. If a perfect match cannot be found, doctors can use a donor that is not as closely matched. Cord blood transplants are less likely to cause graft-versus-host disease than are bone marrow transplants. Also, cord blood may be more readily available than bone marrow. Cord blood can be preserved for years. However, bone marrow is generally given fresh or is frozen for a short period of time until the patient is ready to receive it. Cord blood has been used for transplants since 1988.

PERIPHERAL BLOOD

A peripheral blood stem cell transplant involves taking the patient's own blood or a donor's blood. There are far fewer stem cells in circulating blood than in bone marrow or cord blood. Because so few stem cells are in the bloodstream, donors receive a medication for several days before the donation. The medication coaxes the bone marrow into producing and releasing a greater number of stem cells. A special machine filters the donor's blood to remove just the stem cells. The rest of the blood is returned to the donor. The entire process can take four to six hours. The stem cells are given to the patient immediately or are frozen until the patient is ready to receive them.

THE TRANSPLANT PROCESS

Stem cells are amazing. A relatively small number of them can repopulate the bone marrow. Once healthy new stem cells move into the marrow, they immediately begin producing the cells that turn into red blood cells, white blood cells, and platelets. Stem cells from bone marrow, cord blood, and peripheral blood are collected in very different ways. But the process for transplanting the stem cells into the leukemia patient is the same regardless of how the stem cells were obtained.

PREPARATION

Once the doctor is certain of a well-matched stem cell donor, he prepares the patient for the transplant. Before the transplant, the doctor may use high doses of chemotherapy to destroy the patient's bone marrow. Some patients also receive body-wide radiation to destroy leukemia cells before the transplant. The radiation oncologist (a doctor who specializes in radiation therapy) places lead shields over the lungs, the heart, and the kidneys to protect them from the radiation.

This preparation not only destroys cancer cells, but it also weakens the immune system. This reduces the risk of the patient rejecting the transplanted stem cells. (Rejection is not an issue with autologous transplants in which the stem cells come from the patient's own body.) The preparation temporarily leaves patients with virtually no immune system until the transplant takes place. This may cause life-threatening infections, bleeding, and other problems caused by very low blood cell counts. The days immediately before and after a stem cell transplant are perhaps the most dangerous for leukemia patients.

RECEIVING THE TRANSPLANT

The transplant itself is surprisingly simple. The stem cells are just like blood, whether they came from bone marrow, cord blood, or peripheral blood. The patient receives the stem cells through a large intravenous line. It takes one to six hours. Remarkably, the transplanted stem cells know just where to go. They make their way to the bone marrow and settle in. If everything goes right, the stem cells begin creating new bone marrow and new stem cells. It may take several weeks for the blood count—the red and white blood cells and the platelets—to start increasing.

Patients may have to remain in the hospital for three to five weeks, sometimes longer. Some patients go home sooner, but they require frequent monitoring. Doctors must take repeated blood tests and occasional bone marrow biopsies to check the patient's progress. It can take a full year for the blood count and immune system to return to normal. In the meantime, patients may need blood and platelet transfusions.

SIDE EFFECTS AND COMPLICATIONS

Stem cell transplants cure many people of their leukemia and put others into long-lasting remissions. A few people develop leukemia again because the preparation period may not have killed every leukemia cell. This is more likely to happen with an autologous transplant than an allogeneic transplant. Autologous transplant complications may include bacterial, fungal, and viral infections; complications of the gastrointestinal tract and liver; and problems with the brain or the lungs. These problems are related to side effects of the preparation—damaged cells and a depressed immune system.

A common complication specific to patients who receive allogeneic stem cell transplants is graft-versus-host disease. The immune system cells from the donor recognize the patient's body as being foreign. The donor immune system cells—which are much stronger than the patient's own immune system—attack the patient's body just as if they were fighting an infection. The liver, the skin, and the gastrointestinal tract are most often affected. The risk of graft-versus-host disease increases with the degree of HLA mismatch. There is also a higher chance of this happening among older donors and patients. Graft-versus-host-disease can be treated with steroids and other medications. In the worst cases, it is deadly to the patient.

Other times, the patient's immune system recognizes the donor stem cells as foreign and rejects the transplanted cells. This is called graft rejection. By the time patients receive donor stem cell transplants, they have little or no bone marrow of their own left. If a patient's body rejects the stem cell transplant, he will not be able to make any blood cells at all. This is one reason why the patient's immune system is purposely destroyed prior to the transplant. Since the patient has no functioning immune system, it cannot reject the transplanted stem cells.

STEM CELL CONTROVERSY

The success of stem cell transplants has prompted some parents of children with leukemia to conceive siblings for the purpose of becoming donors. A naturally conceived sibling has a one in four chance of being a very good HLA match for its older sibling. But those odds may not be good enough for parents of children who can die without a matched stem cell transplant.

Modern technology allows for better chances of a sibling match. Embryos can be conceived in a laboratory by removing eggs from the mother and fertilizing them with the father's sperm. The embryos are microscopically small balls of cells that are a few days old. They have not yet developed organs such as hearts or brains. When technicians find an embryo that is a genetically good match to the sick brother or sister, the doctor implants that embryo into the mother's womb. This selection process is called preimplantation genetic diagnosis. When the infant is born, its cord blood may save its older sibling's life. If the sibling needs further treatment in the future, the new child could also be a matched bone marrow or a peripheral stem cell donor.

This process, as with stem cell research in general, is very controversial. The embryos that do not match are usually destroyed or turned over for medical research. People who are against this process believe that embryos are babies. They say that destroying an embryo is the same as killing a baby. They also worry that a young child cannot give informed consent to be a donor for an older sibling later on.

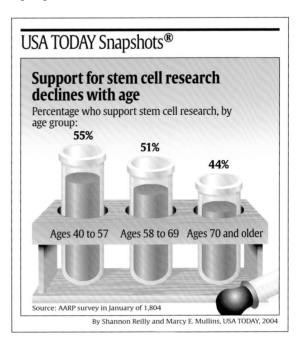

USA TODAY Snapshots®

Support for stem cell research declines with age

Percentage who support stem cell research, by age group:

55% — Ages 40 to 57
51% — Ages 58 to 69
44% — Ages 70 and older

Source: AARP survey in January of 1,804

By Shannon Reilly and Marcy E. Mullins, USA TODAY, 2004

www.usatoday.com

News
SECTION A

June 4, 1991

From the Pages of USA TODAY

Toddler may be sister's lifesaver

LOS ANGELES - At 13 months, Marissa Eve Ayala is too young to know that she gets a chance to save her big sister's life. That's what she was born to do.

In what has become a controversial case, doctors at City of Hope National Medical Center will extract bone marrow from her tiny pelvic bones. The marrow will be transfused into Marissa's 19-year-old sister, Anissa, who is dying of chronic myelogenous leukemia.

The sisters' parents, Mary and Abe Ayala conceived Marissa in hope she would be a compatible donor. Neither parent nor their other child was a suitable match. They have rejected criticism that Marissa would be a "medicine chest baby" saying instead that she was a "blessing from God."

The Ayalas had tough odds to beat before Marissa was born. First, Abe Ayala had to get his vasectomy reversed. Then Mary Ayala had to get pregnant and bear a healthy child at age 43. Lastly, Marissa's marrow had to match Anissa's. "The Ayalas certainly hoped for a possible marrow match but that's not an exclusive reason why they decided to have another child," says City of Hope's Charles Mathews.

Some medical ethicists are troubled by the trend of parents having babies to save other, sick children. "Can parents give informed consent for one child when the recipient is another child?" asks Arthur Caplan, director of the University of Minnesota Center for Biomedical Ethics. "I think we should have a third party approve these cases." The third party would represent a child designated to donate organs or tissue to a sick sibling and a judge would rule on each case, Caplan says.

But Michael Josephson of Joseph and Edna Josephson Institute for Ethics in Marina Del Rey, Calif., says parents like the Ayalas "who are loving enough to go through what they did are most certainly going to be loving, caring parents to this child."

—Sally Ann Stewart

Other people do not believe that a ball of cells with no heart or brain is a baby. And they believe it is ethically acceptable to conceive one child for the purpose of saving another child. Some families say they had planned on having another baby anyway. Why not have one that is genetically matched so that it can help its older sibling?

More patients than ever are surviving leukemia and enjoying normal or near-normal lives. Read on to learn more about how people live with leukemia and the challenges they face. Learn about clinical trials and the promising research being done to find better ways to treat leukemia.

HIS OWN CURE

Michael's CLL went into remission after several rounds of chemotherapy. He felt good enough to resume teaching and running. But the doctors said the chemo was not a cure. Because of his relatively young age, doctors recommended that Michael consider a bone marrow transplant. "That's the irony," Michael said. "I was in remission and feeling great. Then I had to decide to go through hell and risk dying from the procedure rather than just the disease." He decided to go ahead with the transplant. He had no matched siblings. Doctors decided to try what was then a newly developed transplant method that used stem cells from Michael's own body. They gave him an autologous stem cell transplant.

Michael Billig's stem cell transplant has kept him cancer-free since 1999.

USA TODAY

LIVING WITH LEUKEMIA

Aubrey Williams was nine years old when her doctor drove to her house one night to talk to her family. A blood test showed that Aubrey had leukemia. "I felt numb," said Aubrey's mother, Amy Williams. "I know I must have been in shock because I was shaking." A friend of Amy's, who was a nurse, was visiting that night. She urged Amy to take Aubrey to St. Jude Children's Research Hospital. Mother and daughter drove through an ice storm and arrived in Memphis, Tennessee, where St. Jude is located, at four o'clock the next morning. Aubrey's father, who had been traveling on business, met them at the hospital.

The leukemia specialist diagnosed Aubrey with acute lymphocytic leukemia and put her on an intensive course of chemotherapy to rid her body of the cancer. Aubrey's parents moved into housing near St. Jude so they could be close to Aubrey during the treatment. Even though Aubrey had a good response to chemotherapy, the doctors said she would need two to three years of treatment. Leukemia cells had entered her spinal canal, so she received chemotherapy into her spine every few weeks. She spent nearly a year at St. Jude, part of the time living with her family.

While an estimated 12,840 people died of leukemia in 2010, more people than ever before survived. The five-year survival rate counts people who are alive five years after being diagnosed with leukemia. Since 1960 the five-year survival rate for all leukemia patients has nearly quadrupled. During the period from 1999 to 2006, the five-year survival rates for the four primary types of leukemia were these:

- Acute lymphocytic leukemia—66 percent for all patients, 91 percent for children under five
- Acute myeloid leukemia—24 percent for all patients, 61 percent for children under fifteen

- Chronic lymphocytic leukemia—80 percent
- Chronic myeloid leukemia—55 percent

Currently, nearly 260,000 people in the United States are in remission from leukemia or are being treated for it. People are being diagnosed with leukemia earlier. This allows treatment to begin as soon as possible. And better treatments allow many people with leukemia to live longer. Wider use of stem cell transplants means that more people than ever before will have a complete recovery. Others may be in remission for many months or even years. People living with leukemia share the same challenges as most other cancer patients.

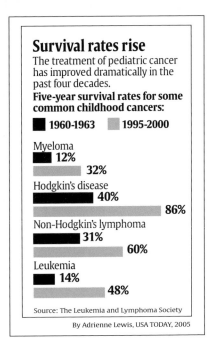

Survival rates rise
The treatment of pediatric cancer has improved dramatically in the past four decades.
Five-year survival rates for some common childhood cancers:
■ 1960-1963   ▨ 1995-2000

Myeloma
■ 12%
▨ 32%
Hodgkin's disease
■ 40%
▨ 86%
Non-Hodgkin's lymphoma
■ 31%
▨ 60%
Leukemia
■ 14%
▨ 48%

Source: The Leukemia and Lymphoma Society
By Adrienne Lewis, USA TODAY, 2005

LIVING WITH LEUKEMIA

When doctors tell people they have leukemia, it affects their family members and friends as well. People with leukemia may go through denial, anger, depression, hopelessness, and fear. All are normal emotions for anyone faced with a serious illness. At this point, patients and families often want to learn everything they can about leukemia. Many people mistakenly believe that getting leukemia is an automatic death sentence. If they investigate potential treatments, they learn that is not true. Modern treatments can cure or prolong life for nearly everyone with leukemia.

www.usatoday.com

Life
SECTION D

February 22, 2010

From the Pages of USA TODAY

For young cancer patient, a prom night to remember

Hospital stages dance to give Ashley Riemer a little bit of normalcy

*N*ormalcy. That was the word mentioned by friends, family and medical staff at Walter Reed Army Medical Center Saturday night when all eyes were on a beautiful 17-year-old high school senior from Alexandria, Va., who celebrated her "prom" at the Washington, D.C. hospital.

There was an Oscar-night feel in the air as Ashley Riemer—resplendent in a one-shoulder turquoise gown, silver sandals and painted fingers and toes—stepped from a shiny, chauffeured white Lincoln and was

Patients treated at large cancer centers have an important resource available to them. Such centers have teams of doctors, nurses, social workers, and psychologists. These professionals work together to develop the best treatment plan for each patient. Also, the medical staff at a large cancer center is more familiar with the complexities of leukemia treatment.

Treatment for leukemia can be grueling. Chemotherapy, repeated bone marrow biopsies, and frequent blood tests are difficult. However, medications can control side effects such as nausea and vomiting. Patients may miss out on doing the everyday things we take for granted. Cancer hospitals do what they can to help fill that loss. Hospitals often provide recreational activities for patients.

escorted up red-carpeted steps by her stepfather, U.S. Army Sgt. 1st Class Troy Dennison, decked out in full military dress.

Ashley's smile was ear-to-ear and her eyes glistened as cameras clicked and about 60 of her friends from Mount Vernon High School—all dolled up in their senior prom best—cheered, whistled and called out "We love you, Ashley."

Ashley, who has acute myeloid leukemia, has been unable to attend school. She has spent most of that time at Walter Reed undergoing chemotherapy and fighting infections. Her illness put many normal passages of senior year on hold— football games, dances, nights out with friends. When it became clear she was too sick to attend a regular senior prom, those who knew her decided to bring the prom to her.

Plans snowballed from what was going to be a little dance with a jukebox and snacks, to a full-out formal party with a live DJ and catered food. With the help of the non-profit Santa's Foundation, which coordinates charitable events for children with parents in the Armed Forces, the prom grew into a glittering party. Ashley and her parents entered the dance hall and took in the twinkling lights and shimmering star-shaped balloons. Tables were festooned with sapphire blue tablecloths and music vibrated around them.

Ashley's friends were delighted for their pal. They say it has been a hard school year, but Ashley's not a complainer. In an interview a few days before the prom, Ashley echoed words other cancer patients have used. "You realize who your real friends are. I've grown away from some friends and others have stuck by."

—*Mary Brophy Marcus*

Children have playtime and playrooms managed by specialists in childhood development. Teachers may visit hospitals to help these children keep up with schoolwork.

After an initial period of hospitalization, many people receive the rest of their treatment as outpatients. Some patients need to stay near the hospital if they require frequent treatments. Others return home and visit the hospital or the clinic once a week or once a month. Children who are doing well with their treatment may return to school. Adults who work may return to their jobs when they feel well enough.

People completing treatment for leukemia may have conflicting emotions. They will be relieved to have finished what has been a

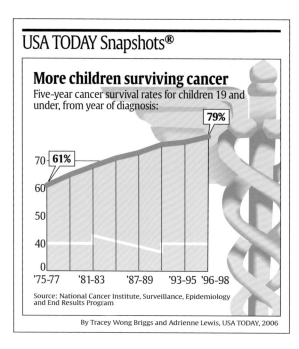

USA TODAY Snapshots®

More children surviving cancer

Five-year cancer survival rates for children 19 and under, from year of diagnosis:

79%

61%

70
60
50
40
0

'75-77   '81-83   '87-89   '93-95 '96-98

Source: National Cancer Institute, Surveillance, Epidemiology and End Results Program

By Tracey Wong Briggs and Adrienne Lewis, USA TODAY, 2006

very challenging period of their lives. They may fear that their leukemia will return. People who are in remission or who have been cured still need to see their doctors for years. Follow-up exams are the only way to detect a possible recurrence of leukemia. Exams also allow doctors to monitor and manage possible long-term effects of treatment.

LIFESTYLE CHANGES

People being treated for a life-threatening illness such as leukemia often think about what they've done with their lives. They may wonder if they've always made the best choices in the past. This can be a good time to take steps to improve health. Some people decide to stop smoking or to eat a healthier diet. Others decide they need to exercise more or to stop drinking alcohol.

DIET AND NUTRITION

It's important for everyone to follow a healthy diet and to eat the right foods. That includes eating well-balanced meals that are low in fat, sugar, and salt. Whole grain bread, cereal, and pasta, along with a wide assortment of fruits, nuts, and vegetables, make up a healthy diet.

But eating right can be tricky for people undergoing cancer treatment. People who receive chemotherapy or radiation often develop nausea and lose their appetite. Radiation can cause pain and sores in the mouth. Medication can make food taste odd. It is common for people undergoing cancer treatment to lose weight. These problems usually disappear when the treatment is over.

People may need to change their eating habits while being treated for leukemia. Eating five to six small meals each day may be easier than eating three big meals a day. Eating very small amounts every couple of hours helps to decrease nausea. A dietitian can help people select foods that are nutritious and easy to eat.

FATIGUE

Severe fatigue may be the most common problem for people being treated for leukemia. Because of the frequent visits to doctors and clinics for treatment, the ongoing worry, the side effects of treatment, and the immune system's constant fight against the leukemia—it's no surprise that fatigue goes along with cancer treatment. Fatigue may continue for a long time after treatment is over.

Doing everyday things can be difficult. People with cancer-related fatigue can learn to manage what energy they have. For example, many people feel better in the morning. They have less fatigue early in the day and more in the afternoon. Morning might be the best time to go shopping, keep medical appointments, visit friends, or go to the park or the zoo. Children might be able to attend school for part of the day.

It is a good idea to spread activities out over the day or even several days. A person with fatigue related to cancer treatment probably will not want to visit the doctor and shop for groceries the same morning. That may even be too much to do in one day. Instead, it might be better to map out the week's activities to conserve energy.

For some people, fatigue comes on suddenly. They must stop what they are doing and lie down. Many people learn to make time for an afternoon nap. A nap of only thirty minutes can be a big energy booster.

EXERCISE AND WEAKNESS

People might wonder why they should exercise when they already feel tired and weak. But for many people, exercise is one of the best things they can do for their health. Exercise generally helps people feel better. It even may improve their response to cancer treatment. Most people will be able to perform some kind of exercise. Exercise has many positive effects for leukemia patients:

- reduce fatigue
- strengthen muscles
- improve cardiovascular fitness
- decrease anxiety and depression
- improve feelings of self-worth and happiness

People who are being treated for leukemia or who are recovering from it should check with their doctors before starting an exercise program. If the doctor approves, it's best to start out with five to ten minutes of exercise. Gradually increase the time over a period of weeks. The American Cancer Society recommends that adults should exercise thirty minutes or more at least five days a week. Children and teens should exercise sixty minutes a day at least five days a week. People with leukemia may not be able to exercise this much at first, but it serves as a goal.

An exercise plan should include both aerobic and weight-bearing workouts. Aerobic exercise includes brisk walking, swimming, bicycling (either a regular bike or a stationary one), and using a treadmill or similar equipment. Aerobic exercise strengthens the heart and lungs. It may also help the immune system to work better.

Weight-bearing exercise builds bone and muscle. People often lose strength and muscle mass because of cancer treatments. Leukemia patients may spend a great deal of time in bed, especially when starting treatment. This causes even more loss of strength and muscle. So it's important to rebuild strength and muscle as soon as possible. Weight-bearing exercise can be as simple as lifting a few barbells or free weights at home. It can be as elaborate as going to a gym and working out with a trainer on sophisticated weight machines.

EMOTIONAL HEALTH

People being treated for leukemia or recovering from it will want to include loved ones in their lives. This is the time to rely on family and friends for comfort and support. Church groups, spiritual advisers, and professional counselors can help. Organizations such as the American Cancer Society, and the American Leukemia and Lymphoma Society offer online support groups. Those same organizations also provide community-based support groups so people can meet in person. Sharing emotions with others going through the same problems can help a lot. Over time, most people learn to cope with their illness and adjust to its limitations.

Many people are interested in trying alternative treatments to improve their mental and physical well-being. This includes treatments such as acupressure, acupuncture, massage therapy, and aromatherapy. Learning relaxation techniques, meditation, and guided imagery also can help. Guided imagery is the process of using thoughts to focus and guide the imagination. It's based on the concept that the body and the mind are connected. Using all the senses, the body responds as though what is imagined is real. For example, people with leukemia might visualize their immune systems successfully killing off leukemia cells.

The Cost of Cancer

Cancers such as leukemia cost the nation about $264 billion in 2010. This includes direct and indirect costs. Direct costs are the cost of medical care itself. Indirect costs include time the survivors lost from work and the lost income from people who died during their careers. For example, say a man earns $40,000 a year. He would have retired at the age of sixty-five, but he died of cancer when he was fifty. He and his family lost the equivalent of fifteen years of salary, approximately $600,000.

An estimated fifty-one million Americans have no health insurance, and millions more do not have enough insurance. Cancer treatments such as stem cell transplants are extremely expensive. That's one reason why communities often hold fund-raising events for families hit by leukemia and other kinds of cancer.

But cancer is not just about money. It's the second-leading cause of death in the United States after heart disease. Cancer causes about one out of every four deaths in the United States. That adds up to approximately 1,500 people each day. Although childhood cancer is rare, it's the second most common cause of death in children after accidents.

Cancer has a devastating impact on patients and their families and friends. But more than fourteen million Americans have survived cancer. Due to better treatments and earlier diagnosis, the number of people living five years or more after diagnosis continues to rise.

Having good emotional health goes a long way toward achieving the best possible physical health. When the mind and the body work together to fight leukemia, a person feels more in control of his or her life. A more positive emotional outlook has the potential to improve cancer treatment outcomes.

CLINICAL TRIALS FOR LEUKEMIA

Some leukemia patients may have tried all the treatments available to them. Or perhaps the patient has had a relapse or did not respond to the first treatment. These patients may wish to take part in investigational studies called clinical trials. These studies allow patients to try drugs and treatments that are not yet approved for general use. These trials may offer the last hope for very sick patients who cannot be helped in other ways.

A clinical trial is a research study that uses human volunteers to find out how well new medications and treatments work. The U.S. Food and Drug Administration (FDA) is the agency responsible for making sure that new treatments are safe and effective. A new treatment must undergo a series of rigorous tests before the FDA approves it for widespread use. People who participate in clinical trials sign papers saying they understand the potential risks and the possible benefits of a new treatment.

Government organizations (for example, the National Institutes of Health), medical institutions (such as large cancer treatment centers), health foundations (for example, the American Cancer Society), and pharmaceutical companies that develop new medications work together on clinical studies. All new medications must be approved by the FDA before they can be used in the United States. The FDA reviews the results of clinical trials to determine if they will approve it. Clinical trials consist of four phases.

USA TODAY

www.usatoday.com
USA TODAY
Life
SECTION D

December 12, 2005

From the Pages of USA TODAY

Assault on blood cancer:

Drug/vaccine strategy attacks stubborn cells

Sometimes, a wonder drug isn't good enough. Doctors and patients around the world hailed the approval of Gleevec in 2001. Scientists engineered Gleevec to silence growth signals from a rogue protein that causes the blood cancer. Patients who were bedridden returned to normal—often staying in remission for years, says Brian Druker, a professor at Oregon Health & Science University.

Yet while Gleevec can keep cancer at bay, it doesn't appear to cure anyone. Patients who stop taking the drug soon relapse. And even apparently healthy patients still harbor hidden reservoirs of cancer. Researchers now are searching for ways to eliminate these stubborn cancer cells.

One experimental method is designed to work with Gleevec like a combined air and ground assault. The strategy aims to boost patients' immune systems to recognize and kill cancer cells. Although scientists still don't completely understand how the immune system fights cancer, they suspect that the body's natural defenses routinely clean up abnormal cells such as cancers. But because tumors arise from the body's own tissues, experts believe the immune system can't always recognize them as a threat.

Therapeutic vaccines, unlike traditional vaccines that prevent diseases, aim to educate the immune system. In a study, scientists injected Gleevec patients with peptides (pieces of proteins) that are found in chronic myeloid leukemia but nowhere else. Scientists hope this may help the body recognize the protein fragments as foreign. The body's guardians may then search out and destroy any cells bearing those peptides.

Druker says the results are promising. After treatment, sophisticated tests were unable to detect any signs of leukemia in six of 18 patients. Earlier cancer vaccines have had mixed success, perhaps because the immune system was overwhelmed by large tumors. Vaccines may work better after drugs such as Gleevec have cut cancers down to a manageable size.

—*Liz Szabo*

Phase 1   Is the medication safe? Researchers test an experimental drug for the first time in a small group of healthy people (twenty to eighty) to evaluate its safety, determine the right dosage, and identify side effects.

Phase 2   Does the medication work? A slightly larger group of people (one hundred to three hundred) take the experimental drug to see if it is effective against the target disease and to further evaluate its safety.

Phase 3   How does it compare with existing medications? Larger groups of people (one thousand to three thousand) take the drug to confirm its effectiveness, monitor side effects, compare it to commonly used treatments, and to collect information that will allow the drug to be safely used.

Phase 4   Are there other potential uses for this medication? Are there any long-term adverse effects? The new drug or vaccine is approved for use. Information continues to be collected as more and more people take the medication over a longer period.

The FDA lists clinical trials on its website at www.clinicaltrials.gov. The government monitors ninety thousand or more clinical trials at any one time. The website allows people to search for clinical trials for specific medical conditions. Many leukemia studies involve giving various combinations of existing medications in different ways or at different times during the course of the disease. A few examples of clinical trials for the treatment of leukemia include these:

- Looking for genetic changes in patients with ALL to help predict which treatments will work best
- Collecting and storing blood and bone marrow from a large number of patients with acute and chronic leukemia for future study

- Identifying people at risk for developing CLL through genetic studies of patients who have that form of leukemia
- Giving combination chemotherapy to young patients who have Down syndrome and AML
- Studying how stem cell transplants affect adolescent and young adult survivors of childhood leukemia

Leukemia remains a very serious disease. However, with the rapid advances in treatments such as targeted medications and stem cell transplants, it is likely that more and more people will conquer leukemia and go on to live normal lives. Scientists are working hard to discover the secrets of human genetics. Leukemia starts with the mutation of a single gene. A mutated gene is like a misspelled word in the middle of a sentence. Fix the word, and the sentence will be correct. Fix the gene, and the person will be healthy. And one day, scientists may develop a vaccine or a similar treatment that prevents leukemia entirely.

HOW ARE THEY DOING?

What happened to the leukemia patients introduced earlier in the text? Read on for updates (as of early 2011).

Shannon Tavarez received an umbilical cord blood stem cell transplant in August 2010. Shannon died of her leukemia three months later. Her new friend and supporter, Rihanna, tweeted, "Just got off a plane and got the horrible news that our little star Shannon Taverez has lost her battle against leukemia" and "Way too soon."

Dominic Mott is in the third grade now and has showed no signs of leukemia since his bone marrow transplant. In January of 2011, Dominic got to meet his bone marrow donor, Kevin Brewster. Dominic's family calls Brewster a hero.

Julian McCann recovered from his leukemia after receiving a bone marrow donation from his brother and is doing well.

Jake Owen is taking the medication that keeps his leukemia under control. He is also doing well.

Yvonne Schmidt will need to take her medication for at least two years to make sure her leukemia does not return. She has returned to many of her usual activities.

Montana Oatman received his last chemotherapy in June 2010 and is doing very well. It took thirty-two months of treatment to cure his leukemia.

Michael Billig recovered from his leukemia and is a professor of anthropology at Franklin and Marshall College in Pennsylvania. He volunteers with a Leukemia and Lymphoma Society program that puts new leukemia patients in touch with survivors.

Aubrey Williams is back home with her family. She still takes a chemotherapy pill once a day and has weekly intravenous chemotherapy. She needs a few more months of medication and tests. She goes to school most days and is expected to recover fully. She wants to be a nurse when she grows up.

USA TODAY

GLOSSARY

acute leukemia: a rapidly progressing cancer that starts in the bone marrow. The disease causes large numbers of abnormal white blood cells to be produced and enter the blood stream.

acute lymphocytic leukemia (ALL): a fast-growing type of leukemia in which too many lymphoblasts (immature white blood cells) are found in the blood and bone marrow; also called acute lymphoblastic leukemia

acute myeloid leukemia (AML): a fast-growing type of leukemia in which too many immature white blood cells other than lymphocytes are found in the blood and bone marrow; also called acute myelogenous leukemia

allogeneic stem cell transplant: a procedure in which a person receives blood-forming stem cells from a genetically similar, but not identical, donor; may be a sibling or an unrelated donor

anemia: a condition in which the number of red blood cells is below normal

antibodies: proteins made by the immune system that attack and destroy microbes that invade the body. Each antibody is specific to each antigen.

antigen: protein substances that cause an immune reaction in the body; includes bacteria, viruses, and even pollen

apoptosis: the self-destruction of damaged or sick cells; stops mutations from being passed on to the next generation of cells

autologous stem cell transplant: a procedure in which blood-forming stem cells are removed, treated, and later returned to the same person

B cell: a white blood cell that comes from bone marrow; part of the immune system, makes antibodies to help fight infections; also called B lymphocyte

benzene: a chemical that is used widely by the chemical industry; also found in tobacco smoke, vehicle emissions, and gasoline fumes. Exposure to it may increase the risk of developing leukemia.

biopsy: the removal of cells or tissue for examination by a pathologist

blast: an immature blood cell that cannot function normally

blood: a tissue with red blood cells, white blood cells, platelets, and other substances suspended in fluid called plasma; carries oxygen and nutrients to tissues; carries away wastes

blood-brain barrier: network of blood vessels with closely spaced cells that makes it difficult for bacteria and potentially toxic substances (such as anticancer drugs) to enter the brain

bone marrow: the soft, spongelike tissue in the center of most bones. Yellow marrow is mostly fat. Red marrow produces white blood cells, red blood cells, and platelets.

bone marrow aspiration: removal of a small sample of liquid bone marrow (usually from the hip) through a needle for examination under a microscope; helps doctors to know what kind of leukemia a patient has

bone marrow biopsy: removal of a larger amount of bone and bone marrow through a bigger needle for examination under a microscope; helps doctors to know what kind of leukemia a patient has; helps to determine how treatment is helping

bone marrow transplant: a procedure to replace bone marrow after it has been destroyed by high doses of chemotherapy or radiation. A transplant may be autologous or allogeneic.

cell: the individual unit that makes up the tissues of the body. All living things are made up of one or more cells.

cerebrospinal fluid (CSF): the fluid that flows through the brain and along the spinal cord to help protect and cushion it

chemotherapy: a treatment with strong medications that kill leukemia cells

chromosome: part of a cell that contains genetic information. Human cells contain forty-six chromosomes in twenty-three pairs (except for sperm and eggs, which contain just twenty-three).

chronic leukemia: a slowly progressing cancer that starts in blood-forming tissues of the bone marrow; causes large numbers of white blood cells to be produced and enter the bloodstream

chronic lymphocytic leukemia (CLL): a slow-growing type of leukemia in which too many lymphoblasts (immature white blood cells) are found in the blood and bone marrow; also called chronic lymphoblastic leukemia

chronic myeloid leukemia (CML): a slowly progressing disease in which too many white blood cells other than lymphocytes are made in the bone marrow; also called chronic myelogenous leukemia

clinical trials: formal research studies that test how well new medical treatments or medications work in people

complete blood count (CBC): a blood test to check the number of red blood cells, white blood cells, and platelets in a sample of blood

consolidation therapy: a type of high-dose chemotherapy given as the second phase (after induction therapy) of cancer treatment for leukemia

CT scan (computed tomography scan): a series of detailed pictures of areas inside the body taken from different angles. The pictures are created by a computer linked to an X-ray machine.

DNA (deoxyribonucleic acid): the genetic information that determines how our bodies look and work; the information that makes us what we are

Down syndrome: a disorder caused by an extra chromosome 21; characterized by mental retardation and distinguishing physical features. For unknown reasons, Down syndrome increases the risk of leukemia.

Gleevec: the brand name for imatinib, a drug to treat chronic myeloid leukemia

graft-versus-host disease (GVHD): caused when transplanted stem cells (the graft) attack the host (the patient's immune system)

hematologist: a doctor who specializes in treating leukemia and other blood disorders

hemoglobin: a substance inside red blood cells that binds to oxygen and carries it from the lungs to the tissues

human leukocyte antigens (HLA): certain types of proteins found on the surface of most cells. Stem cell transplants require the closest possible HLA match between donor and recipient to work.

human T-cell leukemia virus type I (HTLV-1): a virus that infects T cells (a type of white blood cell) and can cause leukemia; can be spread by sharing syringes or needles, through blood transfusions, sexual contact, and from mother to child during birth or breast-feeding

imatinib: a drug most often used to treat chronic myeloid leukemia; blocks the protein made by a mutated oncogene; a type of tyrosine kinase inhibitor; also called by the brand name Gleevec

immune system: the complex group of organs and cells that defends the body against infections and other diseases such as leukemia

induction therapy: the first phase of treatment for leukemia. The goal is to achieve a remission with no leukemia cells in the bone marrow and a normal blood count.

interferon: a natural immune system protein used to help the body's immune system. Laboratories produce large amounts of synthetic interferon to treat leukemia and other cancers.

intrathecal chemotherapy: a treatment in which anticancer drugs are injected into the fluid-filled space between the thin layers of tissue that cover the brain and the spinal cord

leukapheresis: a process of temporarily removing huge numbers of abnormal white blood cells before or during treatment for leukemia

leukemia: cancer that starts in the blood-forming tissue of the bone marrow; causes large numbers of abnormal white blood cells to be produced and enter the bloodstream

lymph: the clear fluid that travels through the lymphatic system

lymphatic system: a system composed of vessels, lymph, and lymph nodes; an important part of the immune system

lymph nodes: masses of lymphatic tissue that are part of the lymphatic system. They collect bacteria, viruses, cancer cells, and help to destroy them.

maintenance therapy: treatment given to help the original treatment keep working; used to help keep leukemia in remission

monoclonal antibody: a type of protein made in the laboratory that locates and binds to leukemia cells; can be very effective with fewer side effects than chemotherapy

mutation: permanent changes in a cell's DNA; can be caused by many factors such as ultraviolet radiation, cigarette smoke, chemicals; can be inherited

myeloid leukemia: a form of leukemia that affects stem cells of the bone marrow that make red blood cells, platelets, and certain white blood cells; may also be called myelogenous or myelocytic leukemia; can be acute or chronic

oncogene: a gene that promotes growth of cancer cells

oncologist: a doctor who specializes in tumors

pathologist: a doctor who identifies diseases by studying cells and tissues under a microscope

peripheral blood: blood circulating throughout the body

peripheral stem cell transplant: a method of collecting stem cells in the circulating blood as a form of leukemia treatment. Collected stem cells are given to the patient after radiation has destroyed the bone marrow. This helps the bone marrow recover and start producing healthy blood cells. This may be the only possible cure for some leukemia patients.

Philadelphia chromosome: an abnormality of chromosome 22 in which part of it is swapped with part of chromosome 9. This abnormal chromosome is found in most cases of chronic myeloid leukemia and occasionally in other forms of leukemia.

platelets: fragments of certain cells produced in the bone marrow. They help prevent bleeding by causing blood clots to form.

proto-oncogenes: genes that promote and regulate normal cell division

radiation therapy: the use of high-energy radiation from X-rays, gamma rays, neutrons, protons, and other sources to kill leukemia cells and shrink enlarged organs such as spleens

red blood cell (RBC): a cell that carries oxygen to all parts of the body; also called erythrocyte

relapse: the return of signs and symptoms of leukemia after a period of improvement

remission: decrease in or disappearance of leukemia symptoms, although leukemia cells still may be in the body

risk factor: something that increases the chance of developing a disease such as leukemia. Examples include: age, family history, smoking, exposure to radiation or certain chemicals, and genetic mutations.

side effect: a problem that occurs when treatment such as chemotherapy or radiation affects healthy tissues or organs; includes fatigue, pain, nausea, vomiting, decreased blood cell counts, hair loss, and mouth sores

spinal tap: a procedure in which a needle is put into the lower part of the spinal column to collect cerebrospinal fluid or to give drugs; also called lumbar puncture

spleen: an organ located on the left side of the abdomen that is part of the lymphatic system; filters the blood, stores blood cells, and destroys old blood cells

stem cell: a cell from which other types of cells develop. In the bone marrow, all blood cells develop from stem cells.

stem cell transplant: giving stem cells to a patient after leukemia treatment to help the bone marrow recover so it can start producing healthy blood cells

targeted therapy: a type of treatment that uses drugs or other substances, such as monoclonal antibodies, to find and attack specific cancer cells; usually less toxic than chemotherapy with fewer side effects

T cell: a white blood cell that attacks virus-infected cells, foreign cells, and cancer cells; also produces substances that regulate the immune response; also called T lymphocyte

thymus gland: a gland in the middle of the chest that is part of the immune system; large in children, very small in adults

transfusion: taking blood or blood components such as platelets from a healthy person and putting it into a patient's veins; may be used to treat leukemia when the red blood or platelet count is low

translocation: movement of one part of a chromosome to another during cell division; a translocation resulting in the Philadelphia chromosome is the primary cause of AML

tumor lysis syndrome: a side effect of chemotherapy in which the drugs kill so many white blood cells that the body cannot cope with the cellular waste products; may lead to kidney failure or irregular heartbeats

tumor suppressor genes: genes that slow down cell division; may delay division until a cell has repaired its damaged DNA; may trigger apoptosis—cellular suicide—if DNA cannot be repaired

tyrosine kinase: an abnormal protein associated with the Philadelphia chromosome; allows leukemia cells to reproduce without control

tyrosine kinase inhibitors: medications that block tyrosine kinase; slows or stops leukemia cells from splitting

umbilical cord blood: blood from the umbilical cord of a newborn baby and its mother's placenta. This blood contains high numbers of stem cells.

umbilical cord blood transplant: giving stem cells collected from umbilical cord blood and placentas to patients after leukemia treatment; helps the bone marrow recover so it can start producing healthy blood cells; increasingly used in leukemia patients as a replacement for bone marrow transplants

vaccine: medications given to prevent infections; in cancer treatment, used to stimulate the immune system so that it will recognize and help fight leukemia and other cancer cells

white blood cells (WBCs): blood cells other than red blood cells or platelets; WBCs called lymphocytes come from lymphoid stem cells; other WBCs (neutrophils, eosinophils, and macrophages) come from myeloid stem cells. WBCs are formed in the bone marrow. WBCs are abnormal in most forms of leukemia.

RESOURCES

American Cancer Society (ACS)
http://www.cancer.org
800-ACS-2345

The American Cancer Society is the leading national voluntary health organization dedicated to eliminating cancer as a major health problem by preventing cancer, saving lives, and diminishing suffering from cancer, through research and education. People can reach volunteers at the ACS twenty-four hours a day, seven days a week to answer questions about cancer. The service also answers e-mails from cancer patients and their families. On the website, you can search for information about cancer. Click on "choose a cancer topic" and the type of leukemia you want to know about.

Centers for Disease Control and Prevention (CDC)
1600 Clifton Road Atlanta, GA 30333
http://www.cdc.gov/cancer/skin/
800-CDC-INFO

The CDC's mission is to promote health and quality of life by preventing and controlling disease, injury, and disability among Americans. The CDC conducts research to develop methods to better identify, control, and cure diseases. Search under hematologic (blood) cancers for information about the different forms of leukemia. People may contact the CDC twenty-four hours a day, seven days a week.

Leukemia and Lymphoma Society (LLS)
1311 Mamaroneck Avenue
White Plains, NY 10605
http://www.leukemia-lymphoma.org
800-955-4572

The Leukemia and Lymphoma Society is committed to providing information, support, and guidance to people living with leukemia and other blood disorders. The information specialists (social workers and health educators) provide up-to-date disease and treatment information. They can help patients and families to communicate with their health-care teams and can locate information about clinical trials.

National Cancer Institute
NCI Office of Communications and Education, Public Inquiries Office
6116 Executive Boulevard, Suite 300
Bethesda, MD 20892-8322
http://www.cancer.gov
800-4-CANCER

This organization is part of the U.S. government's National Institutes of Health. It coordinates the National Cancer Program, which conducts and supports research, training, education, and other programs about the causes, diagnosis, prevention, and treatment of cancer. The site offers a authfree online chat with cancer information specialists.

SOURCE NOTES

10 Nicole Johnson, "Young Broadway Star Fights Leukemia," *My Fox New York*, June 16, 2010, http://www.myfoxny.com/dpp/news/local_news/young-broadway-star-fights-cancer-20100616 (February 25, 2011).

20 Gina Kim, "Donor Meets 10-Year-Old Whose Life He Saved," *Sacramento Bee*, January 7, 2011, http://www.sacbee.com/2011/01/07/3305922/bakersfield-bone-marrow-donor.html#ixzz1CBKI20Ct (February 25, 2011).

33 Ibid.

34 Kaitlyn Lionti, "Hundreds Gather to Benefit for Town of Tonawanda Family," *Buffalo YNN*, June 7, 2010, http://buffalo.ynn.com/content/all_news/509387/hundreds-gather-to-benefit-for-town-of-tonawanda-family/?ap=1&MP4 (February 25, 2011).

41 David J. Hill, "Ken East Goes Bald for Bucks," *Tonawanda News*, April 29, 2010, http://tonawanda-news.com/local/x537288767/Ken-East-goes-Bald-for-Bucks (February 25, 2011).

42 Michael E. Young, "Injury Leads to Royse City Baseball Player's Early Cancer Diagnosis," *Dallas Morning News*, May 10, 2010, http://www.dallasnews.com/sharedcontent/dws/news/localnews/stories/051010dnmetbaseballkid.3dec77f.html (February 25, 2011).

42–43 Ibid.

53 Ibid.

54 Hank Long, "In Sickness and Health," *South Washington County Bulletin*, April 1, 2010, http://m.swcbulletin.com/article.cfm?id=14991&tag=Lifestyle (February 25, 2011).

69 Ibid.

70 St. Jude Children's Research Hospital, "Montana, Patient of the Month, April 2009," April 2009, http://www.stjude.org/stjude/v/index.jsp?vgnextoid=9d1 23dc49d910210VgnVCM1000001e0215acRCRD&vgnextchannel=60780d1e ea46e110VgnVCM1000001e0215acRCRD (February 25, 2011).

70 Ibid.

85 Alison Johnson, "The Giving Spirit," *Health Journal*, December 2009, http://www.thehealthjournals.com/archive.php?id=488 (March 23, 2011).

86 Bill Glovin, "To Hell and Back with My Cousin Michael," *Hopkins Medical News*, Fall 1999, http://www.hopkinsmedicine.org/hmn/F99/top.html (February 25, 2011).

97 Scott C. Anderson, "The New Bone Marrow Transplants," *Science for People*, January 5, 2003, http://www.scienceforpeople.com/Essays/NewBMT.htm (February 25, 2011).

98 St. Jude Children's Research Hospital, "Aubrey, Patient of the Month, May 2010," St. Jude Children's Research Hospital, May 2010, http://www.stjude. org/stjude/v/index.jsp?vgnextoid=5c0082887b148210VgnVCM1000001e02 15acRCRD&vgnextchannel=b75c170ae9395210VgnVCM1000001e0215acRC RD (February 25, 2011).

110 Robyn Rihanna Fenty, "@rihanna," November 2, 2010, http://twitter.com/#!/ rihanna (March 15, 2011).

SELECTED BIBLIOGRAPHY

American Cancer Society. "Cancer Facts & Figures." 2010. http://www.cancer.org/acs/groups/content/@epidemiologysurveilance/documents/document/acspc-026238.pdf. (October 2010).

———. "Childhood Leukemia." 2009. http://www.cancer.org/Cancer/Leukemiain-Children/DetailedGuide/index. (October 2010).

———. "Leukemia—Acute Lymphocytic in Adults." 2009. http://www.cancer.org/Cancer/Leukemia-AcuteLymphocyticALLinAdults/DetailedGuide/index (September 2010).

———. "Leukemia—Acute Myeloid (Myelogenous). 2010. http://www.cancer.org/acs/groups/cid/documents/webcontent/003110-pdf.pdf (July 2010).

———. "Leukemia—Chronic Lymphocytic). 2010. http://www.cancer.org/Cancer/Leukemia-ChronicLymphocyticCLL/DetailedGuide/index (September, 2010).

———. "Leukemia—Chronic Myeloid (Myelogenous). 2010. http://www.cancer.org/Cancer/Leukemia-ChronicMyeloidCML/DetailedGuide/leukemia-chronic-myeloid-myelogenous-what-is-c-m-l (September 2010).

Bartley, Karen, Catherine Metayer, Steve Selvin, Jonathan Ducore, Patricia Buffler. "Diagnostic X-rays and Risk of Childhood Leukemia." *International Journal of Epidemiology*. 39, no. 6 (2010): 1,628–1,637.

Beck, Melinda. "What It Takes to Become a Living Donor," *Wall Street Journal*. http://online.wsj.com/article/SB10001424052748704905004575405233300863958.html, (August 3, 2010).

Bozzone, Donna M. *The Biology of Cancer: Leukemia*. New York: Chelsea House, 2009.

Lerner, Adrienne W, ed. *Perspectives on Diseases and Disorders: Leukemia*. Farmington Hills, MI: Greenhaven Press, 2009.

Leukemia & Lymphoma Society. "Acute Lymphocytic Leukemia." 2010. http://www.leukemia-lymphoma.org/all_page?item_id=7049 (September 2010).

———. "Acute Myeloid Leukemia." 2010. http://www.leukemia-lymphoma.org/all_page?item_id=8459 (September 2010).

———. "Chronic Lymphocytic Leukemia." 2010. http://www.leukemia-lymphoma.org/all_page?item_id=8501 (September 2010).

———. "Chronic Myelogenous Leukemia." 2010. http://www.leukemia-lymphoma.org/all_page?item_id=8501 (September 2010).

———. "Leukemia Facts & Statistics." 2009. http://www.leukemia-lymphoma.org/all_page?item_id=9346 (July 2010).

National Cancer Institute. "Biological Therapies for Cancer." NCI. June 13, 2006, http://www.cancer.gov/cancertopics/factsheet/Therapy/biological (February 25, 2010).

———. "What You Need to Know about Leukemia." NCI. November 25, 2008. http://www.cancer.gov/cancertopics/wyntk/leukemia (May 2010).

Nelson, Rebecca. "History of Leukemia." Rebecca Lee Nelson Jacobs. http://rebec-canelson.com/leukemia/history.html (October 2010).

Sawyers, C.L. "Even Better Kinase Inhibitors for Chronic Myeloid Leukemia." *New England Journal of Medicine* 362, no. 24 (2010): 2,314–2,315.

FURTHER READING AND WEBSITES

Books

Ball, Edward D. *100 Q&A about Leukemia.* Sudbury, MA: Jones and Bartlett Publishers, 2007. Read about leukemia from a doctor's and a patient's perspectives.

Keene, Nancy. *Childhood Leukemia: A Guide for Families, Friends & Caregivers.* Sebastopol, CA: Patient Centered Guides, 2010. This guide tells the families of young leukemia patients what to expect and how to cope with leukemia, including personal stories and advice from parents of other patients.

Picoult, Jodi. *My Sister's Keeper.* New York: Simon and Schuster, 2004. In this novel, Anna was conceived to be a bone marrow and blood donor for her older sister who has leukemia. Now at thirteen years old, she takes on her parents in a legal battle to gain control over her body and to what extent it's used to prolong her sister's life.

Silverstein, Alvin, Virginia Silverstein, and Laura Silverstein Nunn. *Cancer: Conquering a Deadly Disease.* Minneapolis: Twenty-First Century Books, 2006. Read more about the causes of cancer, the symptoms, and the treatments in this informational book for young adults.

Takayuki, Ishi. *One Thousand Paper Cranes: the Story of Sadako and the Children's Peace Statue.* New York: Laurel Leaf, 2001. The middle-grade story of Sadako Sasaki, her battle with leukemia following an atomic bomb explosion, and her paper cranes has earned widespread fame.

Winner, Cherie. *Circulating Life: Blood Transfusion from Ancient Superstition to Modern Medicine*. Minneapolis: Twenty-First Century Books, 2007. This book explores the components of blood and the history of blood transfusions, with fascinating facts and lots of photos.

Websites

Bone Marrow Foundation
http://www.bonemarrow.org/

The site offers extensive information about bone marrow transplants and donations. This organization can help provide funding for expensive bone marrow transplants and can sponsor fund-raising activities for individuals. Patients and their families can contact the foundation with questions and can join an online support group. The site lists bone marrow transplant centers across the United States and gives information on family housing.

Clinical Trials
http://www.clinicaltrials.gov

Maintained by the National Institutes of Health, this site is a registry of clinical trials conducted in the United States and around the world. It provides information about a trial's purpose, who may participate, locations, and phone numbers. Thousands of trials are listed. You can search for studies about leukemia.

CureSearch National Childhood Cancer Foundation
http://www.curesearch.org/

CureSearch National Childhood Cancer Foundation is dedicated to raising private funds for childhood cancer research for the Children's Oncology Group, the world's largest cooperative cancer research organization. They are committed to conquering childhood cancer through scientific discovery and compassionate care.

The National Childhood Cancer Foundation (NCCF) is a nonprofit, public benefit charity dedicated to support research to conquer childhood cancer. The vision of NCCF is to eliminate cancer as the cause of more deaths during childhood than any other disease. NCCF's mission is to support nationwide, multi institution, cooperative research and public policy to benefit children and adolescents with cancer, survivors, and their families.

Hope Street Kids
http://www.hopestreetkids.org/

The mission of Hope Street Kids is to eliminate childhood cancer through pioneering research, advocacy, and education. The site offers information about various kinds of cancer, statistics, diagnosis, and treatment.

National Coalition for Cancer Survivorship
http://www.canceradvocacy.org/toolbox/11-living-beyond-cancer/

This organization is the oldest survivor-led cancer advocacy organization in the country. Among its many resources is a two-hour audio presentation titled "Living Beyond Cancer."

National Marrow Donor Program
http://www.marrow.org/

The site offers information on bone marrow and cord blood transplants. It is a nonprofit organization creating the opportunity for all patients to receive needed transplants. It maintains a registry for potential donors. The registry lists nine million people who have volunteered to donate bone marrow if needed.

St. Jude Children's Research Hospital
http://www.stjude.org

The mission of St. Jude Children's Research Hospital is to advance cures and means of prevention for pediatric diseases through research and treatment. Consistent with the vision of its founder actor Danny Thomas, no child is denied treatment based on race, religion, or a family's ability to pay. St. Jude Children's Research Hospital is internationally recognized for its pioneering work in finding cures and saving children with cancer and other catastrophic diseases. St. Jude is the first and only pediatric cancer center to be designated as a Comprehensive Cancer Center by the National Cancer Institute.

TeensHealth
http://kidshealth.org/teen/

This site is sponsored by the prestigious Nemours Foundation, one of the nation's leading pediatric health-care systems. It has sections for teens, kids, and parents. You can find information about numerous topics such as leukemia and other kinds of cancer, schools, drugs, fitness, and sexual health. Videos give additional information about selected medical tests.

WebMD
http://www.webmd.com

WebMD provides detailed health information on hundreds of topics. All content on the Web is written and reviewed by health-care professionals and is updated frequently. Its mission is to provide objective, trustworthy, and timely health information. Search for information on leukemia in the alphabetical directory or by using the search box.

Expand learning beyond the printed book. Download free, complementary educational resources for this book from our website, www.lerneresource.com

INDEX

ABOUT THE AUTHOR

Connie Goldsmith is a registered nurse with a bachelor of science degree in nursing and a master of public administration degree in health care. She is the author of three USA Today Health Reports: Diseases and Disorders books: *Skin Cancer, Influenza,* and *Hepatitis.* Other books include *Invisible Invaders: Dangerous Infectious Diseases, Meningitis, Cutting-Edge Medicine, Superbugs Strike Back: When Antibiotics Fail,* and *Battling Malaria: On the Front Lines against a Global Killer.* She has published more than two hundred magazine articles, mostly on health topics for adults and children. She also writes a pediatric health column for a regional parenting magazine. She lives near Sacramento, California.

PHOTO ACKNOWLEDGMENTS

The images in this book are used with the permission of: © Steve Gschmeissner/ Science Photo Library/Getty Images, pp. 1, 3, 27 © Laura Westlund/Independent Picture Service, pp. 6, 12, 26, 28, 31; © Robert Hanashiro/USA TODAY, p. 8; © Robert Sabo/New York Daily News/Getty Images, p. 10; © Leslie Smith, Jr./USA TODAY, p. 17; © National Cancer Institute/Photo Researchers, Inc., p. 25; © Biophoto Associates/Photo Researchers, Inc., pp. 37, 45; © Addenbrookes Hospital/Photo Researchers, Inc., p. 39; © Albert T. McCracken, Jr., p. 41; © Camille Tokerud/The Image Bank/Getty Images, p. 43; © Jan Hinsch/Photo Researchers, Inc., p. 47 (left); © Dr. Gopal Murti/Photo Researchers, Inc., p. 47 (right); © Simon Fraser/RVI, Newcastle upon Tyne/Photo Researchers, Inc, p. 50; © Mediscan/Visuals Unlimited, Inc., p. 61; © Paul Gunning/Photo Researchers, Inc., p. 88; © Robert Deutsch/USA TODAY, p. 89; © Michael Billig, p. 97.

Front Cover: © Steve Gschmeissner/Science Photo Library/Getty Images.

Main body text set in USA TODAY Roman 10/15.